THE GOSPELS
IN OUR IMAGE

ALSO BY DAVID CURZON

Midrashim
Modern Poems on the Bible: An Anthology

THE GOSPELS
IN OUR IMAGE

An Anthology of
Twentieth-Century Poetry
Based on Biblical Texts

edited by David Curzon

HARCOURT BRACE & COMPANY
New York   San Diego   London

Library of Congress Cataloging-in-Publication Data
The Gospels in our image: an anthology of twentieth-century poetry based on Biblical texts/edited by David Curzon.—1st ed.
p.   cm.
Includes selections from the Gospels, chiefly in the Revised Standard Version, with a few passages in the King James Version.
Includes bibliographical references and indexes.
ISBN 0-15-100161-8
1. Religious poetry.   2. Christian poetry.   3. Poetry—20th century.
I. Curzon, David.   II. Bible. N.T. Gospels. English.
Revised Standard. Selections.   1995.
PN6110.R4G55   1995
808.81'9382—dc20   95-11011

The text was set in Spectrum.
Designed by Linda Lockowitz
Printed in the United States of America

First edition

A   B   C   D   E

CONTENTS

INTRODUCTION

Do not judge, God! Never
Were you a woman on Earth.
　Marina Tsvetayeva
　from "The Fatal Volume"

He was dying on the cross
on a hospital bed
loneliness stood there by his side
the mother of sorrows
　Anna Kamienska
　from "On the Cross"

THE RESPONSE OF TWENTIETH-CENTURY POETS TO THE GOSPELS

Poets of the twentieth century, like those who lived before them, have responded with imaginative engagement to the Gospel narrative and to the parables and other teachings embedded in it. All poems in this anthology are based directly or indirectly on short passages in the Gospels. Such appropriation of well-known stories and teachings is perhaps the most ancient of literary forms.

Narrative: Modern Magi

Modern poets respond to the Gospel narrative using such literary devices as retelling its stories with a modern emphasis and anachronistic details, adopting a surprising viewpoint, or applying the situations and teachings to themselves or to contemporary circumstances. The main events in the narrative are often treated by focusing on the psychology of the situation or, in the case of the miracles, as opportunities for ironic observations on ordinary life. Many of the poems present sympathetic views of problematic characters such as Martha and Judas, and even of nonhuman characters in the story, such as the donkey on which Jesus rode into Jerusalem, and the barren fig tree that withered when Jesus said "May no fruit ever come from you again."

Poems on the Magi illustrate the wide range of imaginative responses to the Gospel story. T. S. Eliot, for example, in "Journey of the Magi," has one of the Magi speak and tell us what a difficult trip it all was, with "the camel men cursing and grumbling / And running away, and wanting their liquor and women." They were left somewhat puzzled and asked themselves, "were we led all that way for / Birth or Death?" In the end, they had become estranged:

> We returned to our places, these Kingdoms,
> But no longer at ease here, in the old dispensation,
> With an alien people clutching their gods.

Ramon Guthrie, in "The Magi," provides us with other details: the Magi took along with them "slippers and sleeping pills / laxatives lighter fluid flea powder" and so on, and "The one who was fluent in Aramaic asked the shepherds, / Are there in these place one inn?" Boris Pasternak, in "The Christmas Star," has both the shepherds and the Magi appear and request a look at the newborn child, but Pasternak (or rather, Dr. Zhivago, the putative author of the poem) tells us that Mary only allowed the Magi to enter. Bertolt Brecht, in "Mary," offers a revisionist version of events:

> The shepherds' coarse chatter fell silent.
> Later they turned into the Kings of the story.
> The wind, which was very cold
> Turned into the singing of angels.

We may note in support of Brecht's revisionism that there are no "kings" in the text, nor is the number of magi given. All this, as well as their names, are later amplifications, just like the material in the poems collected here.

Jeffrey Fiskin takes an even more political view than Brecht of the Magi and their visit. He opens by stating that "They were kings, after all" and so were drawn by the news of a new power in the region. They offered their gifts for the political purposes normally motivating kings' gifts. But Fiskin characterizes the gifts as "useless" for these purposes and returns in the final couplet of his sonnet to his opening observation, both as a means of formal closure and to emphasize the mistaken motivation of the visit. James Dickey, in "The Magus," uses the first person singular to describe his identification with the Magi while looking at an infant in his crib. The poet asks, "Is this my son, or another's?" and tells us "my face is lit up by his body" like the faces of the Magi in paintings of the Adoration. Sylvia Plath, on the other hand, has "the abstracts" hovering over a crib in her poem "Magi." They are

> The real thing, all right: the Good, the True—

> Salutary and pure as boiled water,
> Loveless as the multiplication table.
> While the child smiles into thin air.

The child is being blessed by abstractions and, as Plath asks, "What girl ever flourished in such company?" Stanisław Barańczak, writing while his native Poland was still under Communist rule, transforms the story quite differently in "The Three Magi." In his fantasy the Magi are coming to arrest an innocent:

> The forceps of the doorbell will pull you out by the head
> from under the bedclothes; dazed as a newborn baby,
> you'll open the door. The star of an ID
> will flash before your eyes.
> Three men. In one of them you'll recognize
> with sheepish amazement (isn't this a small
> world) your schoolmate of years ago.

They will enter and "the smoke from their cigarettes / will fill the room with a fragrance like incense." These are the magi of the Brave New World of Communism, which, it turned out, was not the kingdom of heaven. William Butler Yeats calls the magi of his imagination "the pale unsatisfied ones" who return again and again to the source of their revelation, still

> hoping to find once more,
> Being by Calvary's turbulence unsatisfied,
> The uncontrollable mystery on the bestial floor.

The magi of Yeats were not converted by their visit or by the subsequent events represented by "Calvary's turbulence." But they remain fascinated, nonetheless, by the origins of the "uncontrollable mystery" and all that happened as a result of the birth they celebrated and continue their "pale unsatisfied" hope to find in it the answers they seek.

Similar imaginative responses occur in other narrative sections. For example, in Czeslaw Milosz's "Tempation," his personal Temptations in the Wilderness come as he walks "On a ridge overlooking neon cities, / With my companion, the spirit of desolation." Milosz is applying the Gospel story of the Temptations directly to his own situation, as Dickey and Barańczak do with the Magi story. On the other hand, Zbigniew Herbert, in "Hakeldama," elaborates on the story of Judas itself, as T. S. Eliot, Ramon Guthrie, and Boris Pasternak did with the Magi. Herbert informs us that "The priests have a problem / on the borderline of ethics and accounting." The priests, in Herbert's account, examine various possibilities of "what to do with the silver coins / Judas threw at their feet." They believe

> it wouldn't be right
> to buy a candle holder with it for the temple
> or give it to the poor

He ends with the same solution given in the biblical text. In other poems Zbigniew Herbert also explores lacunae in the original texts. In "Speculations on the Subject of Barabbas," he asks "What happened to Barabbas" and responds "no one knows." The reason for his inquiry turns out to be personal, with the authorial "I" no doubt referring to both the character speaking in the poem and to Herbert himself reflecting on his (and others') behavior in Communist Poland in the years after the Second World War:

> I ask because in a sense I took part in the affair
> Attracted by the crowd in front of Pilate's palace
>   I shouted
> like the others Barabbas let Barabbas free

Again, various possible answers to his question are noted and he concludes with the biblical text and the situation of "the Nazarene." Herbert has shown the reader a contemporary application of this part of the Gospel story, and the lesson is very general: "in a sense I took part in the affair."

Nicanor Parra exhibits a light touch in his elaborations. In "The Anti-Lazarus," the speaker (who sounds very much like Nicanor Parra himself) is a friend of the dead Lazarus, urgently warning him not to come back to life:

> Lazarus
> don't come forth from the grave
> resurrection won't do a thing for you
>
> . . .
>
> your heart was a rubbish heap
> —that's what you wrote—I'm quoting now—
> there was nothing left of your soul
>
> then why come back to Dante's inferno?
> why play the comedy again?

And "The Discourse of the Good Thief," Parra's version of what the Good Thief said from his cross, gives us a portrait of a thief who is immediately plausible:

> Remember me when thou comest into thy Kingdon
> Appoint me President of the Senate
> Appoint me Director of the Budget

Such lighthearted examinations of the story complement some of the weightier and (perhaps) more serious meditations placed next to them. Jorge Luis Borges, for example, makes this assertion about the Good Thief at the end of his poem, "Luke XXIII":

. . . the candor that made him
Ask for and be granted Paradise
From the ignominy of punishment

Was what tossed him many times
To sin, to the blood-stained gamble.

On the subject of the crucifixion, some poets write relatively
traditional descriptions. But many apply the story to other times
and contexts. Thomas Hardy, for example, in "Unkept Good Fri-
days" writes of those unknown martyrs "Whose virtues wrought
their end," in a poem dated "Good Friday, 1927":

No annual Good Fridays
    Gained they from cross and cord,
From being sawn asunder,
    Disfigured and abhorred,
Smitten and trampled under:
    Such dates no hands have scored.

Wilfred Owen, in "At a Calvary near the Ancre," locates the cru-
cifixion on a battlefield during World War I; János Pilinszky, in
"Passion of Ravensbrück," in that death camp; and Anna Kamien-
ska, in what is perhaps the simplest and most powerful transfor-
mation, locates it "on a hospital bed," with the mother of sorrows
being "loneliness":

My God my God
why have you forsaken me

Sudden silence
All had happened
that was to happen
between someone
and God

The poem is dated 8 May 1986, and is the last entry in her
notebook.

Parables: Modern Prodigal Sons

The parables were meant to be directly applied to the lives of listeners. Twenty centuries later many poets prove to be excellent listeners. Jorge Luis Borges, for example, applies the Parable of the Talents rather severely to himself as "the worthless servant" in his poem "Matthew XXV:30":

> In vain have we squandered the ocean on you,
> In vain the sun, seen by Whitman's wonderful eyes;
> You have spent the years and they've spent you,
> And yet you have not written the poem.

The poets' response to the parables, however, is often to the narrative rather than the implicit teaching. They treat the parables as stories and elaborate on them in the same way they elaborate on the stories of the Magi or the crucifixion. The section on the Prodigal Son, for example, contains poems on his departure, on the experiences leading up to his decision to return, and on his return and welcome. The parable is so rich in connotation that each small segment of it is grist for the poets' mills, each sentence a separate source of inspiration. In this, too, the poets are following an age-old tradition of those who have mined the Prodigal Son's story for sermons or political speeches or have used it as material for meditation and application to their own lives.

Rainer Maria Rilke's poem, "The Departure of the Prodigal Son," is an acute and sympathetic dissection of the youthful decision to depart from family and the familiar and go off into the unknown. In Rilke's poem, the phrase "to depart" (or variations on it) is repeated four times. The son is impelled to go away from "all this complication / that's ours without it being our own," away from what "attaches / to us," from the everyday and ordinary "which you no longer really see," from the sorrow "that filled childhood right to the brim,"

> and to depart: but why? from impulse, character,
> impatience, vague anticipation,
> from not perceiving and the unperceived

Elizabeth Bishop joins the Prodigal Son while he is brooding about his return:

> The pigs stuck out their little feet and snored.
> The lantern—like the sun, going away—
> laid on the mud a pacing aureole.
> Carrying a bucket along a slimy board,
> he felt the bats' uncertain staggering flight,
> his shuddering insights, beyond his control,
> touching him. But it took him a long time
> finally to make his mind up to go home.

Edwin Arlington Robinson's Prodigal Son has just come home and is already cajoling his disgruntled elder brother: "You are not merry, brother. Why not laugh, / As I do, and acclaim the fatted calf?" Leah Goldberg has an entire cast waiting at home for the Prodigal Son, with brother, sister, bride, father, and mother all in various emotional states, and the mother explaining

> "Your father will never forgive you
> Who chose the forbidden path.
> But rise and receive the blessing
> Of your father's loving wrath."

Léopold Sédar Senghor's Prodigal Son is returning from Europe to Africa, his feet "caked with the mud of Civilization." Marina Tsvetayeva has him remaining "on the highways"; she tells us that the son returns to his father's house "only in the story." And Ivan Bunin gives us a large generalization of the parable, and a possible intent of the text, in which the Prodigal Son represents the soul after death confronted by a nonjudgmental God making inquiries:

> The time will come, the Lord will ask his prodigal son:
> "In your life on earth, were you happy?"

Direct Teachings: Modern Sermons on the Mount

Some twentieth-century poets have affirmed the teachings of the Gospels by applying them to contemporary situations. Others exhibit ambivalence or opposition, and use distancing wit and irony in their response. Many well-known teachings, such as the Beatitudes, the Lord's Prayer, and the injunctions to love your enemy and turn the other cheek, have provoked poems of strong emotional resistance.

Jorge Luis Borges, in his prose poem "From an Apocryphal Gospel," tackles the Beatitudes head on, producing a series of his own:

7 Blessed is he who insisteth not in being in the right: for no man is wholly in the right.
8 Blessed is he who forgiveth others, and he who forgiveth himself.

Bruce Dawe gives us a series of bureaucratic Beatitudes:

Blessed are the memos from above stamped forthrightly
    in magenta FOR IMMEDIATE ATTENTION
        for they shall receive it;
      . . .
Blessed also the intercom calling this one or that
    from his labours that he may enter into the Presence

Yusef Iman uses the phrase "Love your enemy" as an ironic refrain:

Brought here in slave ships and pitched overboard
Love your enemy
Language taken away, culture taken away
Love your enemy

Iman ends with a question implicit in the extensive evidence that many victims identify all too readily with their oppressors: "Love, for everybody else, / but when will we love ourselves?" Jacob Glatstein, writing in Yiddish in the United States after the Second World War, makes a distinction between two types of enemies. There are those who slap you but at least offer you a chance to turn the other cheek, and there are those who show no such charity. Glatstein's parents were murdered in the Maidenek concentration camp by the second kind of enemy:

> How much Christian, so to speak, can I get?
> . . .
>
> All my face-slappers have slapped both my cheeks.
> Cossacks have never given a Mishnah-Jew[1]
> A chance to turn his other cheek.

Russian poet Leonid Zavalniuk's "I Love My Enemies," in an ironic affirmation of the biblical text, refers to the first kind of enemy:

> You trampled my hopes.
> Who can measure my loss?
> Still, I'm grateful, friend:
> you didn't kill me,
> though you're stronger than I am
> and don't believe in anything at all.

Ted Hughes, in "Crow's Theology," presents Crow as a Manichaean:

> Crow realized there were two Gods—
>
> One of them much bigger than the other
> Loving his enemies
> And having all the weapons.

The Lord's Prayer is often treated by means of transformations. Jacques Prévert, for example, starts his poem "Our Father":

> Our Father who art in heaven
>   Stay there
> And we'll stay here on earth
> Which is so pretty sometimes

and continues by listing the somewhat ambivalent pleasures of life on earth:

> With her good children and bad subjects
>   With all the marvels of the world

                    Which are there
          Simply on the earth
                    Offered to everyone
                    Scattered

and ends, still ambivalent:

                    The pretty girls and the old fools
          With the straw of misery rotting in the steel of cannons.

Stanisław Barańczak uses the Lord's Prayer to formulate a non-believer's need for belief, in "N. N. Tries to Remember the Words of a Prayer":

          Our Father, who art not,
          . . .
          because the world
          goes on without You,
          come into being:
          the man who goes to bed counting
          all his lies, fears, and treacheries of the day,
          all those inevitable and fully justifiable
                    acts of shame,
          must believe You do exist,
          must believe You exist, if he's to sleep
          through yet another night.

César Vallejo, in "Our Daily Bread," ends his poem with an unfulfillable yearning:

          And in this frigid hour, when the earth
          has the odor of human dust and is so sad,
          I wish I could beat on all the doors
          and beg pardon from someone,
          and make bits of fresh bread for him
          here, in the oven of my heart . . . !

And D. H. Lawrence, in "Lord's Prayer," prays with admirable energy and a humility different than Vallejo's, ending with an evocative and strangely appropriate image:

> Give me, Oh give me
> besides my daily bread
> my kingdom, my power, and my glory.
>
> All things that turn to thee
> have their kingdom, their power, and their glory.
> . . .
> Like the power and glory of the goose in the mist
> honking over the lake.

THE POEMS AND THE GENRE

Principles of Selection

This anthology is a collection of twentieth-century poems that appealed to me as being skillful, imaginative, intelligible, and of interest as a response to a Gospel text. These poems seem to me to form a distinct modern literary genre. To be in this genre, it must be possible to read the entire poem as a response to a Gospel text. The genre includes poems leading up to a denouement that uses the text, but excludes those with only a passing allusion to it. It also excludes poems of general meditation on a biblical subject that are not tied to one particular short text. In a few cases the selections do not conform strictly to these rules. Explanations of these selections can be found in the notes at the back of the book. The vast majority of the poems, however, are so closely tied to a biblical text by their titles and overt subject matter that it is not only possible to read the poem as a response to the text, but also to be sure that this is something the poet had in mind. But regardless of the author's intent, knowledge of a specific biblical text is needed to fully appreciate the poems collected here.

I hope this anthology will be of interest both on literary

grounds, prompting readers and writers to think of poems based directly on biblical texts as part of a genre, as well as on religious grounds, as a collection of responses to the content of the Gospels by some of the greatest writers of the century, along with their lesser known contemporaries.

This is not a collection of poems primarily expressing religious beliefs or spiritual sentiments. In fact, some difficulty with the text, some emotional tension, is likely to be the precipitating cause of most responses of literary interest. The scarcity of poems tied to specific biblical texts in existing anthologies of religious poetry led me to realize how far the genre is from conventional notions of the religious.

Over half the poems in the anthology were written in English. Poems originally written in other languages were judged by their qualities in English translation and included only if a good translation was found. Quite a number of new translations were made for this anthology. Information on each poet's nationality and years of birth and death can be found in the index of poets.

In order to adequately represent the work of major poets who have been attracted to the genre, I have included several poems by Rainer Maria Rilke, Boris Pasternak, Czeslaw Milosz, D. H. Lawrence, and Jorge Luis Borges. However, the basis for selection was always the merit of the poem as an example of the genre, not the reputation of the poet. Unfortunately, several poems, including a few that are well-known, had to be dropped from the anthology because of exorbitant permissions costs or legal problems with obtaining permissions, major obstacles for all anthologists of modern poetry.

I made no attempt at systematic coverage of the Gospels. The selection and grouping of poems was determined by the attraction of twentieth-century poets to particular biblical texts, not by religious or scholarly considerations. In sections with more than one poem, I kept in mind complementarities and contrasts when making the final choices. These sections generally start with poems tied most directly to the text, followed by those that make a less direct and more figurative use of it. In some cases, I have arranged the poems to follow the chronological sequence of events in the biblical text.

Intertextuality and the Genre of Midrash

All religious traditions develop a literature of imaginative responses to their sacred canon and interpretive embellishments of it. In recent years literary critics have paid a great deal of attention to the rabbinic version of this art, known by the Hebrew word *midrash*.[2] The characteristics of rabbinic midrash are what I had in mind when putting together an anthology of twentieth-century poems based on the Hebrew Scriptures (the Old Testament)[3], as well as in compiling the present anthology.

Each poem in this anthology is a midrash. Rather than give an abstract definition of the term, I will illustrate it with an example from the Gospels. John 6:31–59 is the report of an extended midrashic sermon by Jesus, preached in the synagogue of Capernaum.[4] It begins:

> So they said to him, "Then what sign do you do, that we may see, and believe you? What work do you perform? Our fathers ate the manna in the wilderness; as it is written [Exodus 16:4, 15; Numbers 11:1–9], 'He gave them bread from heaven to eat.' " Jesus then said to them, "Truly, truly, I say to you, it was not Moses who gave you the bread from heaven; my Father gives you the true bread from heaven. For the bread of God is that which comes down from heaven, and gives life to the world." They said to him, "Lord, give us this bread always." Jesus said to them, "I am the bread of life; he who comes to me shall not hunger, and he who believes in me shall not thirst."

Here Jesus takes up the scriptural reference of his skeptical questioners, generalizes the manna into a symbol of figurative bread from heaven, and then applies this symbol to himself. Such imaginative use of a short biblical text to make a point is a midrash. John 6:42 tells us the point was understood by those listening, and that it disturbed them:

> They said, "Is this not Jesus, the son of Joseph, whose father and mother we know? How does he now say, 'I have come down from heaven?' "

Another midrash of Jesus' is based on Jacob's dream in Genesis 28:12:

> And he dreamed, and behold a ladder set up on the earth and the top of it reached to heaven; and behold the angels of God ascending and descending on it.

John 1:51 reports a quick response by Jesus to a friend of the Apostle Philip's, named Nathaniel. Here, too, Jesus applies the scriptural text to himself in a bold midrash:

> Verily, verily, I say unto you, Hereafter ye shall see Heaven open, and the angels of God ascending and descending upon the Son of Man.

It is important to understand that midrash is both a serious religious and literary genre, and a form of wit. The rabbis of two thousand years ago loved puns. There are puns throughout the rabbinic writings and, for that matter, throughout the book of Genesis. Needless to say, these puns are in Hebrew.

Scholars are uncertain as to whether Jesus spoke Hebrew or Aramaic, a language so close to Hebrew as to be virtually a dialect. But whichever language Jesus spoke, we can be sure he engaged in witticisms and wordplay in it. The passages on the Temptations in the Wilderness, for example, contain quick and witty responses in the midrashic mode:

> And the tempter came and said to him, "If you are the Son of God, command these stones to become loaves of bread." But he answered, "It is written [Deuteronomy 8:3]

'Man shall not live by bread alone,
but by every word that proceeds from
the mouth of God.' "

In the Beatitudes, Jesus echoes Psalm 37:11 ("But the meek shall in-
herit the earth" in the King James Version) and Isaiah 55:1–2 ("to
this man will I look, even unto him that is poor and of a contrite
spirit.") He also engages in wordplay, if not pure pun[5]: "Blessed are
the poor [Hebrew *ani'yim*] in spirit, for theirs is the kingdom of
heaven. . . . Blessed are the meek [Hebrew *anavim*], for they shall
inherit the earth."

Some twentieth-century poets also display their midrashic wit
using wordplay. Mary Fullerton, for example, puns on the text "In
my Father's house are many mansions" (John 14:2) in her poem
entitled "Poetry":

Ecstatic thought's the thing:
Its nature lifts it from the sod.
The father of its soul is God,
And in God's house there are many scansions.

Likewise, Howard Nemerov, in his poem "A Sacrificed Author," is
punning on the text "Father, forgive them; for they know not
what they do" (Luke 23:34):

Father, he cried, after the critics' chewing,
Forgive them, for they know not what I'm doing.

Nemerov's application of Jesus' utterance to a completely unre-
lated situation may provoke the initial reaction that it borders on
the blasphemous. But a moment's reflection will reveal that the
second line is also a theologically orthodox interpretation of the
idea, "they know not what I'm doing, what sacrifice I'm making."
Serious commentary doesn't have to be deadly earnest. Mary Ful-
lerton's poem is also not merely the build-up to a pun, but a care-
fully phrased and serious application of its text. After all, poetry is
a form of inspiration, ecstatic thought that lifts us out of the
mundane.

THE BIBLICAL PASSAGES

Choice and Sequence

There is, of course, a great deal of material common to the four Gospels, raising the question of which Gospel to reproduce alongside the poetry. For many events or teachings, however, only one of the four Gospels contains the text in question: the Prodigal Son is only in Luke, the Magi are only in Matthew, the Wedding at Cana is only in John. In cases where there are two or more versions of an event or teaching but the poet is clearly using details from one particular Gospel, there was also no problem of selection. For the rest, I chose the text that seemed most comprehensive. All parallel texts are cited on the same page. I have kept the biblical passages quoted as short as possible. My aim was to include the main references or allusions found in the poems responding to the given passage, as well as the verses preceding or following these references that were needed to make it reasonably self-contained. Important allusions in the poems to other biblical texts are cited in the Notes section.

There are many English translations of the Bible available that could have been placed opposite the poems. I have used the revised Standard Version (RSV) in this anthology because it is written in a contemporary style that still preserves almost all the phrases and cadences of the King James Version (KJV) that have entered the English literary tradition and are often quoted or alluded to in the poems. In a few sections, the KJV itself is used because the poet is quoting or alluding to phrases not retained in the RSV. These exceptions have been noted in the text. The language in the New Revised Standard Version, published in 1989, while admirable in many respects, seems too far from the KJV's phrasing to be used here.

Another technical issue concerns the sequence in which sections should be presented. Should poems on the Raising of Lazarus (which occurs only in John) precede or follow those on the parable of the Prodigal Son (which is only in Luke)? I chose to follow the chronology of the life of Jesus in *The Oxford Bible Reader's Dictionary and Concordance*.[6]

I have started and ended the anthology with John 1:14 because I wanted to use both poems by Jorge Luis Borges on this verse, one of which takes a prospective view and the other a retrospective view of the text, and because symmetry appeals to me.

Intertextuality in the Gospels

I have reproduced all footnotes in *The New Oxford Annotated Bible* (RSV)[7] that are either alternative translations, alternative or additional texts found in some ancient sources, or citations of passages from the Hebrew Scriptures (Old Testament) that are quoted or alluded to in the Gospel text.

Reference to the Hebrew Scriptures in the Gospels is pervasive. For example, in a literary introduction to the New Testament, Frank Kermode observes that "the last five chapters of Mark contain fifty-seven quotations from, and 160 allusions to, the Old Testament."[8] Rowan A. Greer makes the same point in relation to the infancy stories of Matthew (1:18–2:23), which "are all constructed around prophetic texts."[9] Greer cites Isaiah 7:14 and Micah 5:2 on the birth of the Messiah in Bethlehem; Hosea 11:1 on the flight into Egypt, which also recalls Abraham's flight to Egypt (Genesis 12:10) and the four-hundred-year sojourn of the Israelites there; and Jeremiah 31:15 on the slaughter of the innocents, which recalls the slaughter of Israelite children in Egypt (Exodus 1:22). Similarly, the Magnificat (Luke 1:46–56) closely follows Hannah's song in 1 Samuel 2:1–10, and so on; intertextual references are an integral part of the Gospels, and of critical importance in their interpretation.

The other main aspect of intertextuality in the Gospels concerns different versions of the same event or teaching among the four Gospels. For the start and end points of parallel texts, I have consulted both the annotations in *The New Oxford Annotated Bible* and the material in Throckmorton's *Gospel Parallels: A Synopsis of the First Three Gospels*.[10] I have, however, departed from these scholarly norms whenever the references in the poems seemed to call for it;

in a few places, for example, the Gospel text reproduced ends with a phrase picked up by the poets rather than with the verse terminating that section in the Oxford paragraphing or Throckmorton divisions.

Variations among the Gospels are the main clues used by scholars in trying to understand the sequence in which the Gospels were written and the theological intent of their authors. M. D. Goulder[11] catalogs types of variations among Gospel texts, such as simple transcription (for example, parts of Mark that appear in Matthew), reproduction of prior texts with omissions and abbreviations, explanatory changes, modifications, deliberate change of meaning, and the fusing of stories. Matthew 5:32, for example, modifies Mark 10:11 quite radically:

MARK 10:11	MATTHEW 5:32
Whoever divorces his wife and marries another, commits adultery against her.	Everyone who divorces his wife, except on the ground of unchastity, makes her an adulteress.

Matthew 19:17 is one of Goulder's examples of deliberate changes of meaning, introduced (he speculates) in order to avoid the suggestion in Mark 10:18 that Jesus might have been other than good:

MARK 10:18	MATTHEW 19:17
Why do you call me good? No one is good but God alone.	Why do you ask me about what is good? One there is who is good.

One way of describing what is going on here is to say that Matthew is making midrashic adjustments to Mark. As Daniel Boyarin remarks, "Midrash is best understood as a continuation of the literary activity which engendered the scriptures themselves."[12]

REFERENCES

[1] A simple man whose learning goes beyond the Bible, but who does not reach the level of a scholar.

[2] See, for example, the excellent essays in Geoffrey H. Hartman and Sanford Budick, eds., *Midrash and Literature* (New Haven: Yale University Press, 1986).

[3] David Curzon, ed. *Modern Poems on the Bible: An Anthology* (Philadelphia: The Jewish Publication Society, 1994). A discussion of the characteristics common to the rabbinic midrash and twentieth-century poems based on biblical texts as well as references to guides to the Midrash and to primary and secondary sources in English can be found in the introduction. For an extensive anthology of midrashic poems from all centuries, based on both the Old and New Testaments, see Robert Atwan and Laurance Wieder, eds., *Chapters into Verse: Poetry in English Inspired by the Bible,* 2 vols. (New York: Oxford University Press, 1993).

[4] See the article on "Midrash" in the *Catholic Encyclopedia,* vol. IX (New York: McGraw-Hill, 1967). This article also cites Galatians 4:21–31 and Hebrews 3:7–4:11 and 7:1–10 as examples of midrash in the New Testament.

[5] David Flusser, *Jewish Sources in Early Christianity* (Tel Aviv: MOD Books, 1989), p. 62.

[6] "Christ, Harmony of the Life of," *The Oxford Bible Reader's Dictionary and Concordance* (Cyclopedic Concordance) (Oxford University Press, n.d.), Oxford, pp. 44–52.

[7] Herbert G. May and Bruce M. Metzger, eds., *New Oxford Annotated Bible* (New York: Oxford University Press, 1973).

[8] Frank Kermode, "Matthew," in Robert Alter and Frank Kermode, *The Literary Guide to the Bible* (Cambridge: Harvard University Press, 1987), p. 382.

[9] Rowan A. Greer, "The Christian Bible and Its Interpretation," in James L. Krugel and Rowan A. Greer, *Early Biblical Interpretation* (Philadelphia: The Westminster Press, 1986), p. 135.

[10] Burton H. Throckmorton, Jr., ed., *Gospel Parallels: A Synopsis of the First Three Gospels,* 4th ed. (Nashville and New York: Thomas Nelson Inc., 1979).

[11] M. D. Goulder, chapt. 2, *Midrash and Lection in Matthew* (London: SPCK, 1974).

[12] Daniel Boyarin, *Intertextuality and the Reading of Midrash* (Bloomington: Indiana University Press, 1990), p. 128.

THE GOSPELS
IN OUR IMAGE

THE WORD MADE FLESH

JOHN 1:14

14 And the Word became flesh and dwelt among us, full of grace and truth; we have beheld his glory, glory as of the only Son from the Father.

JORGE LUIS BORGES

John 1:14 (1964)

The oriental histories* relate
That one king of those times, subject to
Splendor and tedium, would venture out alone
And, in secret, wander through the precincts

And lose himself in mobs of people with
rough hands and unknown names;
Today, like that Emir of the Believers,
Harun†, God wants to be with men

And is born of a mother, like the birth
Of dynasties that decompose to dust,
And the whole world will be given up to him,

Air, water, bread, tomorrows, lily, stone,
And afterwards the blood of martyrdom,
The mocking, and the nails, and the beam.

Translated from the Spanish
by David Curzon and Sarah Recalde

*The oriental histories are the stories of the Arabian nights.
† Harun al-Rashid.

D. H. LAWRENCE

Demiurge

They say that reality exists only in the spirit
that corporal existence is a kind of death
that pure being is bodiless
that the idea of the form precedes the form substantial.

But what nonsense it is!
as if any Mind could have imagined a lobster
dozing in the under-deeps, then reaching out a savage and iron
    claw!

Even the mind of God can only imagine
those things that have become themselves:
bodies and presences, here and now, creatures with a foothold in
    creation
even if it is only a lobster on tip-toe.

Religion knows better than philosophy.
Religion knows that Jesus was never Jesus
till he was born from a womb, and ate soup and bread
and grew up, and became, in the wonder of creation, Jesus,
with a body and with needs, and a lovely spirit.

MARINA TSVETAYEVA

The Fatal Volume

The fatal volume
Holds no temptation for
A woman: *Ars Amandi*
For a woman is all of Earth.

The heart is the most faithful
Of all love potions.
From her crib on, a woman
Is someone's deadly sin.

Ah, the sky is too distant!
Lips are closer in the dark.
Do not judge, God! Never
Were you a woman on Earth.

1915

Translated from the Russian
by Nina Kossman

WISŁAWA SZYMBORSKA

Born of Woman*

So that is his mother.
That little woman.
The gray-eyed perpetrator.

The boat in which years ago
he floated to the shore.

Out of which he struggled
into the world,
into non-eternity.

The bearer of the man
with whom I walk through fire.

So that is she, the only one
who did not choose him
ready-made, complete.

Herself she pressed him
into the skin I know,
bound him to the bones
hidden from me.

Herself she spied out
his gray eyes,
with which he looked at me.

So that is she, his alpha.
Why did he show her to me.

Born of woman.
So he too was born.
Born like all others.
Like me who will die.

*A note on this poem can be found on page 267.

The son of a real woman.
A newcomer from body's depths.
A wanderer to omega.

Threatened
by his own non-existence
from all sides
at every instant.

And his head
is a head banging against the wall
that yields but for the moment.

And his movements
are all attempts to dodge
the universal verdict.

I understood
he had already travelled half the way.

But he didn't tell me that,
no, he did not.

"This is my mother,"
was all he said to me.

Translated from the Polish
by Magnus J. Krynski and Robert A. Maguire

THE ANNUNCIATION

LUKE 1:26–38

26 In the sixth month the angel Gabriel was sent from God to a city of Galilee named Nazareth, ²⁷to a virgin betrothed to a man whose name was Joseph, of the house of David; and the virgin's name was Mary. ²⁸And he came to her and said, "Hail, O favored one, the Lord is with you!"^c ²⁹But she was greatly troubled at the saying, and considered in her mind what sort of greeting this might be. ³⁰And the angel said to her, "Do not be afraid, Mary, for you have found favor with God. ³¹And behold, you will conceive in your womb and bear a son, and you shall call his name Jesus.

³²He will be great, and will be called the Son of the Most High;
    and the Lord God will give to him the throne of his father David,
³³and he will reign over the house of Jacob for ever;
    and of his kingdom there will be no end."

³⁴And Mary said to the angel, "How shall this be, since I have no husband?" ³⁵And the angel said to her,

    "The Holy Spirit will come upon you,
    and the power of the Most High will overshadow you;
    therefore the child to be born^d will be called holy,
    the Son of God.

³⁶And behold, your kinswoman Elizabeth in her old age has also conceived a son; and this is the sixth month with her who was called barren. ³⁷For with God nothing will be impossible." ³⁸And Mary said, "Behold, I am the handmaid of the Lord; let it be to me according to your word." And the angel departed from her.

^c Other ancient authorities add *"Blessed are you among women!"*
^d Other ancient authorities add *of you*

ANNA KAMIENSKA

Annunciation

He stood wrapped in air
he said like an angel do not be afraid
then he announced something in a language
which I didn't comprehend
Lord how much we don't understand of the most
     important things
then I remained alone

No one can know
how lonely it is
when an angel departs
the world is then immense open and empty
and the voice cannot describe it
and no hand is friendly enough
words are all mute tied

From now on even an eternity
would be too short for expectation

Translated from the Polish
by David Curzon and Grażyna Drabik

SAMUEL MENASHE

The Annunciation

She bows her head
Submissive, yet
Her downcast glance
Asks the angel, "Why,
For this romance,
Do I qualify?"

STEPHEN MITCHELL

The Annunciation

He tiptoes into the room almost as if he were an intruder. Then
kneels, soundlessly. His white robe arranges itself. His breath
slows. His muscles relax. The lily in his hand tilts gradually
backward and comes to rest against his right shoulder.

She is sitting near the window, doing nothing, unaware of his
presence. How beautiful she is. He gazes at her as a man might
gaze at his beloved wife sleeping beside him, with all the concerns
of the day gone and her face as pure and luminous as a child's
and nothing now binding them together but the sound of her
breathing.

Ah: wasn't there something he was supposed to say? He feels
the whisper far back in his mind, like a mild breeze. Yes, yes, he
will remember the message, in a little while. In a few more
minutes. But not just now.

ROSARIO CASTELLANOS

Nazareth

Descending to the cave where the Archangel
made his announcement, I think
of Mary, chosen vase.

Like any cup, easily broken;
like all vessels, too small
for the destiny she must contain.

Translated from the Spanish
by Magda Bogin

FRANCIS JAMMES

The Five Sorrowful Mysteries

Agony

By the child dying at his mother's side
While other kids play in the pavement below;
By the wounded bird who suddenly falls
And doesn't know how his wing turned to blood;
By burning madness, hunger and thirst;
 Hail Mary!

Scourging

By children beaten when a drunk comes home;
By the donkey whose ribs are constantly kicked;
By the shame the chastised innocent feels;
By the virgin exposed and sold for cash;
By the son whose mother has been reviled,
 Hail Mary!

Crown of Thorns

By the beggar who never had a crown
But those yellow friends, a circle of wasps,
No sceptre but a stick to scare dogs;
By the poet with forehead wreathed in blood
From thorns of impossible desire,
 Hail Mary!

Bearing the Cross

By the old woman staggering under a load
Crying "My God!" By the wretch whose arms
Cannot rest on a human love
As the Son's did on Simon Cyrene;
By the horse fallen under the cart he hauls,
 Hail Mary!

Cruxifixion

By four horizons that crucify the world;
By all whose flesh is torn or succumbs;
By those without feet, by those without hands;
By the sick man whimpering under the knife;
By just men in the ranks of assassins,
    Hail Mary!

Translated from the French
by Jeffrey Fiskin

WILLIAM BUTLER YEATS

The Mother of God⋆

The three-fold terror of love; a fallen flare
Through the hollow of an ear;
Wings beating about the room;
The terror of all terrors that I bore
The Heavens in my womb

Had I not found content among the shows
Every common woman knows,
Chimney corner, garden walk,
Or rocky cistern where we tread the clothes
And gather all the talk?

What is this flesh I purchased with my pains,
This fallen star my milk sustains,
This love that makes my heart's blood stop
Or strikes a sudden chill into my bones
And bids my hair stand up?

⋆A note on this poem can be found on page 267.

PRIMO LEVI

Annunciation

Don't be dismayed, woman, by my fierce form.
I come from far away, in headlong flight;
Whirlwinds may have ruffled my feathers.
I am an angel, yes, and not a bird of prey;
An angel, but not the one in your paintings
That descended in another age to promise another Lord.
I come to bring you news, but wait until my heaving chest,
The loathing of the void and dark, subside.
Sleeping in you is one who will destroy much sleep.
He's still unformed but soon you'll caress his limbs.
He will have the gift of words, the fascinator's eyes,
Will preach abomination and be believed by all.
Jubilant and wild, singing and bleeding,
They'll follow him in bands, kissing his footprints.
He will carry the lie to the farthest borders.
Evangelize with blasphemy and the gallows.
He'll rule in terror, suspect poisons
In spring-water, in the air of high plateaus.
He'll see deceit in the clear eyes of the newborn,
And die unsated by slaughter, leaving behind sown hate.
This is your growing seed. Woman, rejoice.

22 June 1979

Translated from the Italian
by Ruth Feldman and Brian Swann

THE VISIT OF MARY TO ELIZABETH

LUKE 1:39–56

39 In those days Mary arose and went with haste into the hill country, to a city of Judah, ⁴⁰and she entered the house of Zechari'ah and greeted Elizabeth. ⁴¹And when Elizabeth heard the greeting of Mary, the babe leaped in her womb; and Elizabeth was filled with the Holy Spirit ⁴²and she exclaimed with a loud cry, "Blessed are you among women, and blessed is the fruit of your womb! ⁴³And why is this granted me, that the mother of my Lord should come to me? ⁴⁴For behold, when the voice of your greeting came to my ears, the babe in my womb leaped for joy. ⁴⁵And blessed is she who believed that there would be*ᵉ* a fulfilment of what was spoken to her from the Lord." ⁴⁶And Mary said,

"My soul magnifies the Lord,
⁴⁷and my spirit rejoices in God my Savior,
⁴⁸for he has regarded the low estate of his handmaiden.
    For behold, henceforth all generations will call me blessed;
⁴⁹for he who is mighty has done great things for me,
    and holy is his name.
⁵⁰And his mercy is on those who fear him
    from generation to generation.
⁵¹He has shown strength with his arm,
    he has scattered the proud in the imagination of their hearts,
⁵²he has put down the mighty from their thrones,
    and exalted those of low degree;

ᵉ Or believed, for there will be

46–55: The "Magnificat" (so called from the first word of the Latin translation) is based largely on Hannah's prayer in 1 Sam.2.1–10. *Magnifies*, i.e. declares the greatness of.
55: Gen.17.7; 18.18; 22.17; Mic.7.20.

[53]he has filled the hungry with good things,
   and the rich he has sent empty away.
[54]He has helped his servant Israel, in remembrance
   of his mercy,
[55]as he spoke to our fathers,
   to Abraham and to his posterity for ever."
[56]And Mary remained with her about three months,
  and returned to her home.

RAINER MARIA RILKE

Mary's Visitation

At the outset she still carried it quite well
but already, from time to time, when climbing, she
became aware of the marvel of her belly,—
and then she stood, caught breath, up on the high

Judean hills. It was not the land
but her abundance that spread out around her;
going on she felt: you couldn't have more than
the largess that she now perceived.

And it urged her to lay her hand
on the other belly, which was heavier.
And the women swayed toward each other
and touched each other's garb and hair.

Each, filled with her sanctified possession,
had the protection of a woman friend.
In her, the Saviour still was a bud intact,
but the Baptist in the womb of her "aunt"
already leapt, seized with delight.

Translated from the German
by David Curzon and Will Alexander Washburn

STEPHEN MITCHELL

Vermeer

> Quia respexit humilitatem
> ancillae suae. —LUKE 1:48

She stands by the table, poised
at the center of your vision,
with her left hand
just barely on
the pitcher's handle, and her right
lightly touching the windowframe.
Serene as a clear sky, luminous
in her blue dress and many-toned
white cotton wimple, she is looking
nowhere. Upon her lips
is the subtlest and most lovely
of smiles, caught
for an instant
like a snowflake in a warm hand.
How weightless her body feels
as she stands, absorbed, within this
fulfillment that has brought more
than any harbinger could.
She looks down with an infinite
tenderness in her eyes,
as though the light at the window
were a newborn child
and her arms open enough
to hold it on her breast, forever.

DAVID CURZON

A Tour of Ein Kerem*

"There are artifacts from every period here.
This tiny spring, this trickle, is the reason
Ein Kerem was, from Canaanite times on,
always inhabited.   The terraces you see
are very old, perhaps three thousand years.
Two thousand years ago the Virgin came
to freshen up before climbing this hill
on the visit to her cousin St. Luke describes.
That's why the trickle is called Mary's Spring.
And way over there is the valley armies used
as the natural route to take from the coastal plain.
Ein Kerem wasn't in their way and was
too far for an afternoon of rape and looting."

A small source in an untoward location. No wonder
Mary chose this place for her confinement
but left, according to Luke, after three months.

*Ein Kerem (which means "vineyard spring" in Hebrew) is the name of a village on the
outskirts of Jerusalem.

THE NATIVITY

18 Now the birth of Jesus Christ[f] took place in this way. When his mother Mary had been betrothed to Joseph, before they came together she was found to be with child of the Holy Spirit; [19]and her husband Joseph, being a just man and unwilling to put her to shame, resolved to divorce her quietly. [20]But as he considered this, behold, an angel of the Lord appeared to him in a dream, saying, "Joseph, son of David, do not fear to take Mary your wife, for that which is conceived in her is of the Holy Spirit; [21]she will bear a son, and you shall call his name Jesus, for he will save his people from their sins." [22]All this took place to fulfil what the Lord had spoken by the prophet:

[23]"Behold, a virgin shall conceive and bear a son,
    and his name shall be called Emman'u-el"

(which means, God with us). [24]When Joseph woke from sleep, he did as the angel of the Lord commanded him; he took his wife, [25]but knew her not until she had borne a son; and he called his name Jesus.

---

[f] Other ancient authorities read *of the Christ*

21: The Hebrew and Aramaic forms of *Jesus* and *he will save* are similar. The point could be suggested by translating, "You shall call his name 'Savior' because he will save."
22–23: See Is.7.14 n: *Young woman*, Hebrew *'almah*, feminine of *'elem*, young man (1 Sam.17.56; 20.22); the word appears in Gen.24.43; Ex.2.8; Ps.68.25, and elsewhere, where it is translated "young woman," "girl," "maiden."

PHILIP APPLEMAN

Mary

Years later, it was, after everything
got hazy in my head—those buzzing flies,
the gossips, graybeards, hustling evangelists—
they wanted facts, they said,
but what they were really after
was miracles.
Miracles, imagine! I was only a girl
when it happened, Joseph
acting edgy and claiming
it wasn't his baby . . .

Anyway, years later
they wanted miracles, like the big-time cults
up in Rome and Athens, God
come down in a shower of coins,
a sexy swan, something like that.
But no, there was only
one wild-eyed man at our kitchen window
telling me I'm lucky.
And pregnant.
I said, "Talk sense, mister, it's got to be
the one thing or the other."
No big swans, no golden coins
in that grubby mule-and-donkey village. Still,
they wanted miracles,
and what could I tell them? He
was my baby, after all, I washed
his little bum, was I
supposed to think I was wiping
God Almighty?

But they *wanted miracles,* kept after me
to come up with one: "This fellow at the window,
did he by any chance have wings?"
Wings! Do frogs have wings?
Do camels fly?"
They thought it over. "Cherubim," they said,
"may walk the earth like men
and work their wonders."
I laughed in their hairy faces. No
cherub, that guy! But
they wouldn't quit—fanatics, like
the gang *he* fell in with years ago,
all goading him till he began to believe
in quick cures and faith-healing,
just like the cranks in Jerusalem, every
phony in town speaking in tongues
and handling snakes. Not exactly
what you'd want for your son, is it?
I tried to warn him, but he just says,
"I must be about my father's business."
"Fine," I say, "I'll buy you a new
hammer." But nothing could stop him, already
hooked on the crowds, the hosannas,
the thrill of needling the bureaucrats.
Holier than thou, he got, roughing up
the rabbis even. Every night
I cried myself to sleep—my son,
my baby boy . . .

You know how it all turned out, the crunch
of those awful spikes,
the spear in his side, the whole town watching,
home-town folks come down from Nazareth
with a strange gleam in their eyes. Then later on
the grave robbers, the hucksters, the imposters all
claiming to be him. I was sick

for a year, his bloody image
blurring the sunlight.

And now they want miracles, God
at my maidenhead, sex without sin.
"Go home," I tell them, "back to your libraries,
read about your fancy Greeks,
and come up with something amazing, if you must."

Me, I'm just a small-town woman,
a carpenter's wife, Jewish mother, nothing
special. But listen,
whenever I told my baby a fairy tale,
I let him know it was a fairy tale.
Go, all of you, and do likewise.

LUKE 2:1–7

2 In those days a decree went out from Caesar Augustus that all the world should be enrolled. ²This was the first enrollment, when Quirin′i-us was governor of Syria. ³And all went to be enrolled, each to his own city. ⁴And Joseph also went up from Galilee, from the city of Nazareth, to Judea, to the city of David, which is called Bethlehem, because he was of the house and lineage of David, ⁵to be enrolled with Mary, his betrothed, who was with child. ⁶And while they were there, the time came for her to be delivered. ⁷And she gave birth to her first-born son and wrapped him in swaddling cloths, and laid him in a manger, because there was no place for them in the inn.

LOUISE GLÜCK

Nativity Poem

It is the evening
of the birth of god.
Singing &
with gold instruments
the angels bear down
upon the barn, their wings
neither white
wax nor marble. So
they have been recorded:
burnished,
literal in the composed air,
they raise their harps above
the beasts likewise gathering,
the lambs & all the startled
silken chickens. . . . And Joseph,
off to one side, has touched
his cheek, meaning
he is weeping—

But how small he is, withdrawn
from the hollow of his mother's life,
the raw flesh bound
in linen as the stars yield
light to delight his sense
for whom there is no ornament.

RUDYARD KIPLING

A Nativity

1914–18

The Babe was laid in the Manger
    Between the gentle kine—
All safe from cold and danger—
      "But it was not so with mine,
                    (With mine! With mine!)
"Is it well with the child, is it well?"
      The waiting mother prayed.
"For I know not how he fell,
      And I know not where he is laid."

A Star stood forth in Heaven;
    The Watchers ran to see
The Sign of the Promise given—
      "But there comes no sign to me.
                    (To me! To me!)
"My child died in the dark.
      Is it well with the child, is it well?
There was none to tend him or mark,
      And I know not how he fell."

The Cross was raised on high;
    The Mother grieved beside—
"But the Mother saw Him die
      And took Him when He died.
                    (He died! He died!)
"Seemly and undefiled
      His burial-place was made—
Is it well, is it well with the child?
      For I know not where he is laid."

On the dawning of Easter Day
      Comes Mary Magdalene;
But the Stone was rolled away,
      And the Body was not within—

                              (Within! Within!)

"Ah, who will answer my word?"
      The broken mother prayed.
"They have taken away my Lord,
      And I know not where He is laid."

                  . . . . .

"The Star stands forth in Heaven.
      The watchers watch in vain
For Sign of the Promise given
      Of peace on Earth again—

                              (Again! Again!)

"But I know for Whom he fell"—
      The steadfast mother smiled,
"Is it well with the child—is it well?
      It is well—it is well with the child!"

LUKE 2:8–20

8 And in that region there were shepherds out in the field, keeping watch over their flock by night. ⁹And an angel of the Lord appeared to them, and the glory of the Lord shone around them, and they were filled with fear. ¹⁰And the angel said to them, "Be not afraid; for behold, I bring you good news of a great joy which will come to all the people; ¹¹for to you is born this day in the city of David a Savior, who is Christ the Lord. ¹²And this will be a sign for you: you will find a babe wrapped in swaddling cloths and lying in a manger." ¹³And suddenly there was with the angel a multitude of the heavenly host praising God and saying,

¹⁴"Glory to God in the highest,
     and on earth peace among men with whom he is pleased!"⁸

15 When the angels went away from them into heaven, the shepherds said to one another, "Let us go over to Bethlehem and see this thing that has happened, which the Lord has made known to us." ¹⁶And they went with haste, and found Mary and Joseph, and the babe lying in a manger. ¹⁷And when they saw it they made known the saying which had been told them concerning this child; ¹⁸and all who heard it wondered at what the shepherds told them. ¹⁹But Mary kept all these things, pondering them in her heart. ²⁰And the shepherds returned, glorifying and praising God for all they had heard and seen, as it had been told them.

---

⁸ Other ancient authorities read *peace, good will among men*

BERTOLT BRECHT

Mary

The night when she first gave birth
Had been cold. But in later years
She quite forgot
The frost in the dingy beams and the smoking stove
And the spasms of the afterbirth towards morning.
But above all she forgot the bitter shame
Common among the poor
Of having no privacy.
That was the main reason
Why in later years it became a holiday for all
To take part in.
The shepherds' coarse chatter fell silent.
Later they turned into the Kings of the story.
The wind, which was very cold
Turned into the singing of angels.
Of the hole in the roof that let in the frost nothing remained
But the star that peeped through it.
All this was due to the vision of her son, who was easy
Fond of singing
Surrounded himself with poor folk
And was in the habit of mixing with kings
And of seeing a star above his head at night-time.

Translated from the German
by Michael Hamburger and Max Hayward

THE MAGI

MATTHEW 2:1–12

2 Now when Jesus was born in Bethlehem of Judea in the days of Herod the king, behold, wise men from the East came to Jerusalem, saying, [2]"Where is he who has been born king of the Jews? For we have seen his star in the East, and have come to worship him." [3]When Herod the king heard this, he was troubled, and all Jerusalem with him; [4]and assembling all the chief priests and scribes of the people, he inquired of them where the Christ was to be born. [5]They told him, "In Bethelem of Judea; for so it is written by the prophet:

[6]'And you, O Bethlehem, in the land of Judah,

are by no means least among the rulers of Judah;

for from you shall come a ruler

who will govern my people Israel.' "

7 Then Herod summoned the wise men secretly and ascertained from them what time the star appeared; [8]and he sent them to Bethlehem, saying, "Go and search diligently for the child, and when you have found him bring me word, that I too may come and worship him." [9]When they had heard the king they went their way; and lo, the star which they had seen in the East went before them, till it came to rest over the place where the child was. [10]When they saw the star, they rejoiced exceedingly with great joy; [11]and going into the house they saw the child with Mary his mother, and they fell down and worshiped him. Then, opening their treasures, they offered him gifts, gold and frankincense and myrrh. [12]And being warned in a dream not to return to Herod, they departed to their own country by another way.

1: *Herod* the Great died early in 4 B.C. 2: Jer.23.5; Num.24.17.
6: Mic.5.2.

T. S. ELIOT

Journey of the Magi

"A cold coming we had of it,
Just the worst time of the year
For a journey, and such a long journey:
The ways deep and the weather sharp,
The very dead of winter."
And the camels galled, sore-footed, refractory,
Lying down in the melting snow.
There were times we regretted
The summer palaces on slopes, the terraces,
And the silken girls bringing sherbet.
Then the camel men cursing and grumbling
And running away, and wanting their liquor and women,
And the night-fires going out, and the lack of shelters,
And the cities hostile and the towns unfriendly
And the villages dirty and charging high prices:
A hard time we had of it.
At the end we preferred to travel all night,
Sleeping in snatches,
With the voices singing in our ears, saying
That this was all folly.

    Then at dawn we came down to a temperate valley,
Wet, below the snow line, smelling of vegetation;
With a running stream and a water-mill beating the darkness,
And three trees on the low sky,
And an old white horse galloped away in the meadow.
Then we came to a tavern with vine-leaves over the lintel,
Six hands at an open door dicing for pieces of silver,
And feet kicking the empty wine-skins.
But there was no information, and so we continued
And arrived at evening, not a moment too soon
Finding the place; it was (you may say) satisfactory.

All this was a long time ago, I remember,
And I would do it again, but set down
This set down
This: were we led all that way for
Birth or Death? There was a Birth, certainly,
We had evidence and no doubt. I had seen birth and death,
But had thought they were different; this Birth was
Hard and bitter agony for us, like Death, our death.
We returned to our places, these Kingdoms,
But no longer at ease here, in the old dispensation,
With an alien people clutching their gods.
I should be glad of another death.

WILLIAM CARLOS WILLIAMS

The Gift

As the wise men of old brought gifts
    guided by a star
        to the humble birthplace

of the god of love,
    the devils
        as an old print shows
retreated in confusion.

    What could a baby know
        of gold ornaments
or frankincense and myrrh,
    of priestly robes
        and devout genuflections?

But the imagination
    knows all stories
        before they are told
and knows the truth of this one
    past all defection.

The rich gifts
    so unsuitable for a child
        though devoutly proffered,
stood for all that love can bring.
    The men were old
        how could they know

of a mother's needs
    or a child's
        appetite?

But as they kneeled
    the child was fed.
        They saw it
and gave praise!
    A miracle

had taken place,
    hard gold to love,
a mother's milk!
    before
        their wondering eyes.

The ass brayed
    the cattle lowed.
        It was their nature.

All men by their nature give praise.
    It is all
        they can do.

The very devils
    by their flight give praise.
        What is death,
beside this?
    Nothing. The wise men
        came with gift

and bowed down
    to worship
        this perfection.

BORIS PASTERNAK

The Christmas Star*

It was winter. The wind
Blew from the plain.
And the infant was cold
In the cave in the slope of a hill.

The breath of an ox
Warmed him. The livestock
Stood in the cave.
A warm mist drifted over the manger.

Having shaken hay-dust
And grains of millet off their sheepskins,
Shepherds stared sleepily
From a cliff into the midnight distance.

Far off were a snow-covered field,
A graveyard, gravestones, fences,
A cart's shafts in a snowdrift,
And, above the graveyard, a star-filled sky.

---

*A note on this poem can be found on page 267.

And nearby, unseen until then,
More humble than an oil-lamp
In a hut's window, a star
Glimmered over the road to Bethlehem.

It blazed like a haystack, apart
From heaven and God.
Like a reflection from arson,
Like a farmstead or a threshing floor in flames.

It towered like a burning rick
Of hay or straw
In the midst of a universe
Alarmed by this new star.

A growing glow, red above the star,
Was portending something,
And three astrologers hastened
To the call of that unprecedented light.

Behind them trod gift-laden camels;
Harnessed donkeys, each smaller than the one
In front, were going down the hill in little steps.

And all that was to come later
Sprang up far off like a strange vision.
All thoughts of the ages, all dreams, all worlds,
All the future of galleries and museums,
All pranks of fairies, all works of magicians,
All fir trees on earth, all dreams of children.

All the tremor of lighted candles, festoons,
All the splendor of colored tinsel . . .
. . . Even more cruel and furious, the wind blew from the field . . .
. . . All the apples, all the gold glass globes.

Part of the pond was hidden by alder trees,
But, through rooks' nests and treetops,
Part of it was seen quite well from here.

The shepherds could make out clearly
The donkeys and camels plodding along the mill-pond.
—Let's go with everyone and worship the miracle,
They said, closing their coats around them.

Shuffling about in the snow made them warm.
Tracks of bare feet, like sheets of mica,
Led over the bright meadow and behind the hovel.
Sheep dogs growled in the star's light
At the tracks, as at the flame of a candle's stub.

The winter night resembled a fairy tale,
And someone from the snow-covered mountain range
Was constantly mingling, unseen, with the rest.
The dogs wandered, looked back with caution,
And sensed danger, and pressed close to the herdsboy.

Along the same road, through the same land,
Several angels walked with the throng.
Their incorporeality made them invisible,
But each of their steps left a footprint.

A horde of men stood around the rock.
Day was breaking. The trunks of the cedars showed.
—Who are you?—Mary asked them.
—We're a shepherd tribe and envoys from heaven;
We came to sing praises to both of you.
—You cannot all go in. Wait outside.

In the haze before dawn, gray as ashes,
The drovers and shepherds stamped about.
Those who came on foot bickered with riders.
By a log hollowed out for a trough
Camels brayed, donkeys kicked.

Day was breaking. The dawn
Swept the last stars, bits of ashes, from the sky.
Of the vast rabble, Mary allowed
Only the Magi to enter the cleft in the rock.

He slept, all luminous, in the oak manger,
Like a moonbeam in the hollow of a tree.
Instead of a sheepskin, he was warmed
By the lips of a donkey and the nostrils of an ox.

They stood in the shadow, as in the dusk of a barn;
They whispered, groping for words.
Suddenly, in the dark, one touched another
To move him a bit to the left of the manger,
And the other turned: from the threshold, like a guest,
The Christmas star was looking at the Maiden.

Translated from the Russian
by Nina Kossman

WILLIAM BUTLER YEATS

The Magi

Now as at all times I can see in the mind's eye,
In their stiff, painted clothes, the pale unsatisfied ones
Appear and disappear in the blue depth of the sky
With all their ancient faces like rain-beaten stones,
And all their helms of silver hovering side by side,
And all their eyes still fixed, hoping to find once more,
Being by Calvary's turbulence unsatisfied,
The uncontrollable mystery on the bestial floor.

LOUISE GLÜCK

The Magi

Toward world's end, through the bare
beginnings of winter, they are traveling again.
How many winters have we seen it happen,
watched the same sign come forward as they pass
cities sprung around this route their gold
engraved on the desert, and yet
held our peace, these
being the Wise, come to see at the accustomed hour
nothing changed: roofs, the barn
blazing in darkness, all they wish to see.

RAMON GUTHRIE

The Magi

The three wise men looked equivocally
at three different stars.

The one who was fluent in Aramaic asked the shepherds,
"Are there in these place one inn?"

Impious shipwreck.
We had come well supplied
with slippers and sleeping pills
laxatives lighter fluid flea powder
inflatable mattresses and in case of need
a month's supply of prophylactics.

Each saying, "I saw this star and
dropping everything, set out,
sur l'éperon du moment, comme disent les Anglais,
quite unprepared, just as I was."

We found three different Kristkinder
in three different mangers
and went home satisfied
leaving three different infants to make what they might
of frankincense and myrrh.

We have written three different books
all unpublished
each in his own tongue
telling of the hardships and perils of the voyage.

JEFFREY FISKIN

The Magi

They were kings, after all.
Cold, raddled by the wind,
Drilled with foreign sand,
They were political

By blood of birth or war
And so followed the news
Through unexpected snows,
Sheltering among the poor

In rough splintered lofts
Until the first light came
And they at last saw Him
And offered their useless gifts.

They were kings, after all,
Their journey political.

MARINA TSVETAYEVA

Bethlehem

Three kings,
Three coffers,
With precious gifts.

The first coffer—
All the earth,
With its blue seas.

The second coffer:
All of Noah,
All, ark-and-beasts.

Well, and in that one?
What's in the third?
What's in the third, my king?

The king is giving
—Good God!
What's the meaning of this?

The king—steps forward,
The mother—back,
And the baby is crying.

23 November 1921

Translated from the Russian
by Nina Kossman

JOVAN HRISTIĆ

That Night They All Gathered on the Highest Tower

That night they all gathered on the highest tower:
Astronomers, mathematicians, and one of the magi from Syria
To read in the stars the glory of the King of Kings,
And demonstrate his immortality with the aid of geometry.

Just before dawn, they nodded their heads in accord
With one another's interpretations. The answer of the stars
Was positive. The trumpets announced
The glory of the King of Kings to the rising sun.

In the palace, at the table set for the feast, they were awaited
By the one to whom the stars gave their word tonight,
And whose future now overflowed like new wine
Which in the golden chalices awaited the toasts.

Only some youth who had recently mastered geometry,
Was not fully convinced by what was read in the stars,
For the stars always give their answer to mortals
But to what question, only they themselves know.

Translated from the Serbian
by Charles Simic

JAMES DICKEY

The Magus

It is time for the others to come.
This child is no more than a god.

No cars are moving this night.
The lights in the houses go out.

I put these out with the rest.
From his crib, the child begins

To shine, letting forth one ray
Through the twelve simple bars of his bed

Down into the trees, where two
Long-lost other men shall be drawn

Slowly up to the brink of the house,
Slowly in through the breath on the window.

But how did I get in this room?
Is this my son, or another's?

Where is the woman to tell me
How my face is lit up by his body?

It is time for the others to come.
An event more miraculous yet

Is the thing I am shining to tell you.
This child is no more than a child.

SYLVIA PLATH

Magi

The abstracts hover like dull angels:
Nothing so vulgar as a nose or an eye
Bossing the ethereal blanks of their face-ovals.

Their whiteness bears no relation to laundry,
Snow, chalk or suchlike. They're
The real thing, all right: the Good, the True—

Salutary and pure as boiled water,
Loveless as the multiplication table.
While the child smiles into thin air.

Six months in the world, and she is able
To rock on all fours like a padded hammock.
For her, the heavy notion of Evil

Attending her cot is less than a belly ache,
And Love the mother of milk, no theory.
They mistake their star, these papery godfolk.

They want the crib of some lamp-headed Plato.
Let them astound his heart with their merit.
What girl ever flourished in such company?

STANISŁAW BARAŃCZAK

The Three Magi

To Lech Dymarski

They will probably come just after the New Year.
As usual, early in the morning.
The forceps of the doorbell will pull you out by the head
from under the bedclothes; dazed as a newborn baby,
you'll open the door. The star of an ID
will flash before your eyes.
Three men. In one of them you'll recognize
with sheepish amazement (isn't this a small
world) your schoolmate of years ago.
Since that time he'll hardly have changed,
only grown a mustache,
perhaps gained a little weight.
They'll enter. The gold of their watches will glitter (isn't
this a gray dawn), the smoke from their cigarettes
will fill the room with a fragrance like incense.
All that's missing is myrrh, you'll think half-consciously—
while with your heel you're shoving under the couch the book
    they mustn't find—
what is this myrrh, anyway,
you'd have to finally look it up
someday. You'll come
with us, sir. You'll go
with them. Isn't this a white snow.
Isn't this a black Fiat.
Wasn't this a vast world.

Translated from the Polish
by Stanisław Barańczak and Clare Cavanagh

THE MASSACRE OF THE INNOCENTS

MATTHEW 2:16–18

16 Then Herod, when he saw that he had been tricked by the wise men, was in a furious rage, and he sent and killed all the male children in Bethlehem and in all that region who were two years old or under, according to the time which he had ascertained from the wise men. ¹⁷Then was fulfilled what was spoken by the prophet Jeremiah:

> ¹⁸"A voice was heard in Ramah,
> wailing and loud lamentation,
> Rachel weeping for her children;
> she refused to be consoled,
> because they were no more."

18: Quoted from Jer.31.15. *Rachel,* wife of Jacob, died in childbirth and according to Gen.35.16–20 was buried near Bethlehem. *Ramah,* north of Jerusalem, was the scene of national grief (Jer.40.1) inflicted by an enemy.

JULIA HARTWIG

Who Says

While the innocents were being massacred who says
that flowers didn't bloom, that the air didn't breathe bewildering
     scents
that birds didn't rise to the heights of their most accomplished
     songs
that young lovers didn't twine in love's embraces
But would it have been fitting if a scribe of the time had shown
     this
and not the monstrous uproar on a street drenched with blood
the wild screams of mothers with infants torn from their arms
the scuffling, the senseless laughter of soldiers
aroused by the touch of women's bodies and young breasts warm
     with milk
Flaming torches tumbled down stone steps
there seemed no hope of rescue
and violent horror soon gave way to the still more awful
numbness of despair
At that moment covered by the southern night's light shadow
a bearded man leaning on a staff
and a girl with a child in her arms
were fleeing lands ruled by the cruel tyrant
carrying the world's hope to a safer place
beneath silent stars in which these events
had been recorded centuries ago

Translated from the Polish
by Stanisław Barańczak and Clare Cavanagh

A. D. HOPE

Massacre of the Innocents

after Cornelis van Haarlem

The big sweet muscles of an athlete's dream
Pose for the sporting picture; Herod's guard
Opposes the selected Ladies' Team.
The game is Murder, played as a charade.

The white meat of the woman, prime and sleek,
Fends off the bull male from her squealing spawn;
The tenderloin, the buttock's creamy cheek,
Against the gladiator's marble brawn.

This is the classic painter's butcher shop;
—Choice cuts from the Antique—Triumphant Mars
Takes his revenge, the whistling falchions swoop
Round Venus as the type of all mammas.

The game is Nightmare: now, in the grotesque
Abortion of his love-dream, she displays
The pale, ripe carcass of the odalisque,
Now the brood-female in her mastoid grace.

The unruptured egg shrieks in her fallow womb.
Freckled with blood his knife-arm plunges straight
For the fat suckling's throat. He drives it home
Full loaded with his contraceptive hate.

TADEUSZ RÓŻEWICZ

Massacre of the Boys

The children cried "Mummy!
But I have been good!
It's dark in here! Dark!"

See them They are going to the bottom
See the small feet
they went to the bottom Do you see
that print
of a small foot here and there

pockets bulging
with string and stones
and little horses made of wire

A great plain closed
like a figure of geometry
and a tree of black smoke
a vertical
dead tree
with no star in its crown.

[The Museum, Auschwitz, 1948]

Translated from the Polish
by Adam Czerniawski

THE PRESENTATION
IN THE TEMPLE

LUKE 2:21–40

21 And at the end of eight days, when he was circumcised, he was called Jesus, the name given by the angel before he was conceived in the womb.

22 And when the time came for their purification according to the law of Moses, they brought him up to Jerusalem to present him to the Lord [23](as it is written in the law of the Lord, "Every male that opens the womb shall be called holy to the Lord") [24]and to offer a sacrifice according to what is said in the law of the Lord, "a pair of turtledoves, or two young pigeons." [25]Now there was a man in Jerusalem, whose name was Simeon, and this man was righteous and devout, looking for the consolation of Israel, and the Holy Spirit was upon him. [26]And it had been revealed to him by the Holy Spirit that he should not see death before he had seen the Lord's Christ. [27]And inspired by the Spirit[h] he came into the temple; and when the parents brought in the child Jesus, to do for him according to the custom of the law, [28]he took him up in his arms and blessed God and said,

> [29]"Lord, now lettest thou thy servant depart in peace,
>   according to thy word;
> [30]for mine eyes have seen thy salvation
> [31]which thou hast prepared in the presence of all peoples,
> [32]a light for revelation to the Gentiles, and for glory
>   to thy people Israel."

[h] Or *in the Spirit*

22–24: Lev.12.2–8.
23: Ex.13.2,12.

33 And his father and his mother marveled at what was said about him; ³⁴and Simeon blessed them and said to Mary his mother,

"Behold, this child is set for the fall and rising of many in
Israel,
and for a sign that is spoken against
³⁵(and a sword will pierce through your own soul also),
that thoughts out of many hearts may be revealed."

36 And there was a prophetess, Anna, the daughter of Phan'u-el, of the tribe of Asher; she was of a great age, having lived with her husband seven years from her virginity, ³⁷and as a widow till she was eighty-four. She did not depart from the temple, worshiping with fasting and prayer night and day. ³⁸And coming up at that very hour she gave thanks to God, and spoke of him to all who were looking for the redemption of Jerusalem.

39 And when they had performed everything according to the law of the Lord, they returned into Galilee, to their own city, Nazareth. ⁴⁰And the child grew and became strong, filled with wisdom; and the favor of God was upon him.

T. S. ELIOT

A Song for Simeon

Lord, the Roman hyacinths are blooming in bowls and
The winter sun creeps by the snow hills;
The stubborn season has made stand.
My life is light, waiting for the death wind,
Like a feather on the back of my hand.
Dust in sunlight and memory in corners
Wait for the wind that chills towards the dead land.

    Grant us thy peace.
I have walked many years in this city,
Kept faith and fast, provided for the poor,
Have given and taken honour and ease.
There went never any rejected from my door.
Who shall remember my house, where shall live my children's
    children
When the time of sorrow is come?
They will take to the goat's path, and the fox's home,
Fleeing from the foreign faces and the foreign swords.

    Before the time of cords and scourges and lamentation
Grant us thy peace.
Before the stations of the mountain of desolation,
Before the certain hour of maternal sorrow,
Now at this birth season of decease,
Let the Infant, the still unspeaking and unspoken Word,
Grant Israel's consolation
To one who has eighty years and no to-morrow.

    According to thy word.
They shall praise Thee and suffer in every generation
With glory and derision,
Light upon light, mounting the saints' stair.
Not for me the martyrdom, the ecstasy of thought and prayer,
Not for me the ultimate vision.

Grant me thy peace.
(And a sword shall pierce thy heart,
Thine also.)
I am tired with my own life and the lives of those after me,
I am dying in my own death and the deaths of those after me.
Let thy servant depart,
Having seen thy salvation.

THE TEMPTATIONS
IN THE WILDERNESS

MATTHEW 4:1–11
(Parallel texts: Mark 1:12–13; Luke 4:1–13)

4 Then Jesus was led up by the Spirit into the wilderness to be tempted by the devil. ²And he fasted forty days and forty nights, and afterward he was hungry. ³And the tempter came and said to him, "If you are the Son of God, command these stones to become loaves of bread." ⁴But he answered, "It is written,

> 'Man shall not live by bread alone, but by every word that proceeds from the mouth of God.' "

⁵Then the devil took him to the holy city, and set him on the pinnacle of the temple, ⁶and said to him, "If you are the Son of God, throw yourself down; for it is written,

> 'He will give his angels charge of you,'
> and
> 'On their hands they will bear you up,
> lest you strike your foot against a stone.' "

⁷Jesus said to him, "Again it is written, 'You shall not tempt the Lord your God.' " ⁸Again, the devil took him to a very high mountain, and showed him all the kingdoms of the world and the glory of them; ⁹and he said to him, "All these I will give you, if you will fall down and worship me." ¹⁰Then Jesus said to him, "Begone, Satan! for it is written,

> 'You shall worship the Lord your God
> and him only shall you serve.' "

¹¹Then the devil left him, and behold, angels came and ministered to him.

2: Ex.34.28; 1 Kg.19.8.   4: Dt.8.3.   5: *The holy city,* Jerusalem.   6: Ps.91.11–12.
7: Dt.6.16.   10: Dt.6.13.

CZESLAW MILOSZ

Temptation

Under a starry sky I was taking a walk,
On a ridge overlooking neon cities,
With my companion, the spirit of desolation,
Who was running around and sermonizing,
Saying that I was not necessary, for if not I, then someone else
Would be walking here, trying to understand his age.
Had I died long ago nothing would have changed.
The same stars, cities, and countries
Would have been seen with other eyes.
The world and its labors would go on as they do.

For Christ's sake, get away from me.
You've tormented me enough, I said.
It's not up to me to judge the calling of men.
And my merits, if any, I won't know anyway.

Berkeley, 1975

Translated from the Polish
by Czeslaw Milosz and Lillian Vallee

JAMES SIMMONS

In the Wilderness

I sit alone on the rocks trying to prepare
a man to teach what the laws of life are.
Sunlight and silence, nurses against disease,
are busy fighting my infirmities.
The life is simple, you could not say rough,
a stream, some cans and firewood are enough
to live on; but a hostile shift of weather
would bring me sharply up on the short tether
of endurance. We haven't survived by strength alone.
We have neither fur nor fangs. I will go home,
just as I rise from sleep, eat and get dressed.
This is one more resort, not last or best.

A teacher in the wilderness alone
learns to make bread and sermons out of stone.

W. H. AUDEN

from *"The Prolific and the Devourer"*

In these three questions [the three temptations in the wilderness] the whole subsequent history of mankind is, as it were, brought together into one whole, and foretold, as in them are united all the unsolved historical contradictions of human nature. —DOSTOYEVSKY

Command that these stones be turned into bread.

The conversion of stones into bread would be a supernatural miracle. It would mean that there were two sets of laws, the scientific laws of this world and the superior divine laws of a supernatural world.

There is only one way in which stones can be turned into bread, and that is by phantasy, stimulated by hunger. In our popular literature where the scullery maid marries the Prince Charming this and similar miracles are being constantly performed.

Primitive peoples and children begin by thinking that their will is omnipotent. A thing is what I want it to be. *"L'état c'est moi."* They begin with belief, belief in themselves.

They have to be weaned slowly and carefully from this belief for if it is shattered too suddenly, they switch over abruptly from belief in their omnipotence to belief in their absolute impotence: they suffer a psychological trauma and their growth is arrested. For growth consists in the abandonment of belief and the acquisition of faith, and they have only passed from one belief to another.

Satan knows that the miracle is impossible, and hopes by persuading Jesus to attempt it, to destroy his faith in the shock of failure.

If thou be the Son of God, cast thyself down.

Again an attempt to destroy faith by urging the performance of an impossible miracle. The first temptation was the temptation of childhood, this of adolescence.

The child believes in the omnipotence of his sensual desires. As he grows he discovers that this is not so, and becomes conscious of himself as an I separated sharply from the rest of the universe, and further a thinking I, a consciousness to which his physical self is as much an object of thought as are other people and things. For the child's belief in the omnipotence of animal desire, he exchanges a belief in the omnipotence of the intellect: instead of thought being a creation of desire (the phantasy of the universe as bread), matter is a creation of thought. I can throw myself down from the temple because the temple, the street, gravity only exist if I choose to think they do. I can think them away.

Jesus might well have answered the second temptation by reversing his answer to the first: "Man does not live by words alone but by the bread that proceedeth daily from the hand of God. I and my Father are one."

All these will I give thee if thou wilt fall down and worship me.

The first two temptations were concerned with miracles, with belief in the absolute freedom of the will, conceived either as desire or as thought. The last temptation, the temptation of maturity, is concerned, not with Belief but with Faith. Unable to tempt Jesus into false beliefs, Satan appeals to reason.

"Of course," he says, "I never imagined that you would fall for the childish tricks I tried to play on you. You are a grown-up person with a wide experience of the world. And I realise now that you and I are colleagues, who share a common passion for the truth. Like myself you are a person of faith: we both believe that the divine law exists and that it is possible to discover something about it, though we both know that all dogmas and doctrines are at best provisional makeshifts which as time goes on become outmoded and misleading.

"I always tell men, and I expect you do too, not to trust to beliefs and authorities but to search their own experience. 'The Kingdom of Heaven is within you,' I tell them, 'Ask and ye shall receive. Seek and ye shall find.' For there is only one test of the accuracy of our knowledge of the truth, and that is our experience of success or failure. The true Way is the way which works.

"Forgive me if I am boring you with what you know already, but they tell me that you are going round teaching men that the True Way is to love the truth with all their hearts and to love their neighbours as themselves.

"I'm sure they must have muddled the second part of what you said—men never listen properly—for it seems to me to contradict the first. I cannot see how anyone who loves the truth can come to any conclusion but my own, namely, that the True Way is to see that one is stronger than one's neighbour, for the truth is that we love no one but ourselves and hate those who cross our will. That is the divine law and neither you nor I can alter it even if we wanted to, which we don't because we ourselves are subject to that law.

"So if you really did say what I was told you said, I implore you to look again at the world, at human history, in your own heart, and give yourself an honest answer, lest you fall into damnation, for what is damnation but to deny the truth when one has seen it."

In claiming to be able to offer Jesus the Kingdoms of this world, Satan is claiming to be God, for if the Kingdoms of this world are really his, then Jesus is mistaken.

The evidence on which Satan bases his argument may be found in many books, *The Republic, The Prince, Leviathan, Mein Kampf,* but nowhere perhaps more completely and cogently expressed than by the Grand Inquisitor in Dostoyevsky's *The Brothers Karamazov.* Jesus does not answer him, any more than he answered Satan or Pilate, because he does not need to: their own experience answers for them and they know very well what they do, and that they have failed, so that, tormented by the knowledge of failure and of the hate they have aroused, they cry:

"Why dost thou come to hinder us? And why dost thou look

silently and searchingly at me with thy mild eyes? Be angry. I don't want your love."

But had he been listening, not to the Inquisitor himself, but to some attendant who was only repeating his master's words, he might have answered along some such lines as this, taking up the Inquisitor's main arguments in turn.

ZBIGNIEW HERBERT

Mr. Cogito Tells about the Temptation of Spinoza*

Baruch Spinoza of Amsterdam
was seized by a desire to reach God

in the attic
cutting lenses
he suddenly pierced a curtain
and stood face to face

he spoke for a long time
(and as he so spoke
his mind enlarged
and his soul)
he posed questions
about the nature of man

—distracted God stroked his beard

—he asked about the first cause

—God looked into infinity

—he asked about the final cause

—God cracked his knuckles
cleared his throat

when Spinoza became silent
God spake

—you talk nicely Baruch
I like your geometric Latin
and the clear syntax
the symmetry of your arguments

*A note on this poem can be found on page 268.

let's speak however
about Things Truly
Great

—look at your hands
cut and trembling

—you destroy your eyes
in the darkness

—you are badly nourished
you dress shabbily

—buy a new house
forgive the Venetian mirrors
that they repeat surfaces

—forgive flowers in the hair
the drunken song

—look after your income
like your colleague Descartes

—be cunning
like Erasmus

—dedicate a treatise
to Louis XIV
he won't read it anyway

—calm
the rational fury
thrones will fall because of it
and stars turn black

—think
about the woman
who will give you a child

—you see Baruch
we are speaking about Great Things

—I want to be loved
by the uneducated and the violent
they are the only ones
who really hunger for me

now the curtain falls
Spinoza remains alone

he does not see the golden cloud
the light on the heights

he sees darkness

he hears the creaking of the stairs
footsteps going down

Translated from the Polish
by John and Bogdana Carpenter

THE MARRIAGE AT CANA

JOHN 2:1–12

2 On the third day there was a marriage at Cana in Galilee, and the mother of Jesus was there; ²Jesus also was invited to the marriage, with his disciples. ³When the wine gave out, the mother of Jesus said to him, "They have no wine." ⁴And Jesus said to her, "O woman, what have you to do with me? My hour has not yet come." ⁵His mother said to the servants, "Do whatever he tells you." ⁶Now six stone jars were standing there, for the Jewish rites of purification, each holding twenty or thirty gallons. ⁷Jesus said to them, "Fill the jars with water." And they filled them up to the brim. ⁸He said to them, "Now draw some out, and take it to the steward of the feast." So they took it. ⁹When the steward of the feast tasted the water now become wine, and did not know where it came from (though the servants who had drawn the water knew), the steward of the feast called the bridegroom ¹⁰and said to him, "Every man serves the good wine first; and when men have drunk freely, then the poor wine; but you have kept the good wine until now." ¹¹This, the first of his signs, Jesus did at Cana in Galilee, and manifested his glory; and his disciples believed in him.

RAINER MARIA RILKE

On the Marriage at Cana

How could she not take pride in him since he
could make (to her) the plainest things adorned?
Wasn't even the large and lofty night
all in disarray when he appeared?

And didn't that time he got lost
end up, amazingly, a glory of his?
Hadn't the wisest then exchanged
their tongues for ears? Didn't the house

become fresh at his voice? She had
repressed, surely a hundred times,
the display of her delight in him.
She followed him with astonishment.

But at that wedding-feast, there when
unexpectedly the wine ran out,—
she begged him for a gesture with her look
and didn't grasp that he resisted her.

And then he did it. Later she understood
how she had pressured him into his course:
for now he really was a wonder-worker,
and the whole sacrifice was now ordained,

irrevocably. Yes, it was written.
But had it, at the time, as yet been readied?
She: she had driven it forth
in the blindness of her vanity.

At the table piled with fruits and vegetables,
she shared everybody's joy and didn't know
that the water of her own tear ducts
had turned to blood with this wine.

Translated from the German
by David Curzon and Will Alexander Washburn

PETER STEELE

Cana

It might have been a neurotic's paradise,
With all that water there for endless washing,
The catering shaky, and most of us wondering
What sort of promise such a beginning held
For the couple's days and years. And then the wine
Ran out, clean out. What do you say—"One always
Likes to be moderate at these affairs"?—
When what you mean is, "There's more need than they
Can possibly provide for." Anyhow,
After a while they gave us wine in flagons,
The kind of thing it was a privilege
To drink, or think about. I still don't know
Where they had found it, how they bought it, why
They kept it until then. I do remember,
Late in the piece, a man who made some toasts
And drank as if he meant them, and then left,
His mother looking thoughtful: that, and the jars
For water, and the way they seemed to glow.

THOMAS MERTON

Cana

Once when our eyes were clean as noon, our rooms
Filled with the joys of Cana's feast:
For Jesus came, and His disciples, and His Mother,
And after them the singers
And some men with violins.

Once when our minds were Galilees,
And clean as skies our faces,
Our simple rooms were charmed with sun.

Our thoughts went in and out in whiter coats than God's
    disciples',
In Cana's crowded rooms, at Cana's tables.

Nor did we seem to fear the wine would fail:
For ready, in a row, to fill with water and a miracle,
We saw our earthen vessels, waiting empty.
What wine those humble waterjars foretell!

Wine for the ones who, bended to the dirty earth,
Have feared, since lovely Eden, the sun's fire,
Yet hardly mumble, in their dusty mouths, one prayer.

Wine for old Adam, digging in the briars!

ERIC PANKEY

The Reason

To clarify and allow
For abundance, for revery.

To be permitted clemency,
A first, if not a second chance,

A taste, a glimpse, the sleight-of-hand
Of miracles and the obvious.

To see sky, gray and pearl, the jay
Blue in the copper beech, milkweed

Seed stalled in the haze, the wooden
Stairs cracked and sagging, and below

A zinc pail tipped over and spilling
A round pool that reflects the sky.

To take what is closest at hand
And set a story in motion.

Not to make something from nothing,
But, as at Cana, to be moved,

Even unwillingly, by need.

SEAMUS HEANEY

Cana Revisited

No round-shouldered pitchers here, no stewards
To supervise consumption or supplies
And water locked behind the taps implies
No expectation of miraculous words.

But in the bone-hooped womb, rising like yeast,
Virtue intact is waiting to be shown,
The consecration wondrous (being their own)
As when the water reddened at the feast.

NICODEMUS

JOHN 3:1–15

3 Now there was a man of the Pharisees, named Nicode'mus, a ruler of the Jews. [2]This man came to Jesus[d] by night and said to him, "Rabbi, we know that you are a teacher come from God; for no one can do these signs that you do, unless God is with him." [3]Jesus answered him, "Truly truly, I say to you, unless one is born anew,[e] he cannot see the kingdom of God." [4]Nicode'mus said to him, "How can a man be born when he is old? Can he enter a second time into his mother's womb and be born?" [5]Jesus answered, "Truly, truly, I say to you, unless one is born of water and the Spirit, he cannot enter the kingdom of God. [6]That which is born of the flesh is flesh, and that which is born of the Spirit is spirit.[f] [7]Do not marvel that I said to you, 'You must be born anew.'[e] [8]The wind[f] blows where it wills, and you hear the sound of it, but you do not know whence it comes or whither it goes; so it is with every one who is born of the Spirit." [9]Nicode'mus said to him, "How can this be?" [10]Jesus answered him, "Are you a teacher of Israel, and yet you do not understand this? [11]Truly, truly, I say to you, we speak of what we know, and bear witness to what we have seen; but you do not receive our testimony. [12]If I have told you earthly things and you do not believe, how can you believe if I tell you heavenly things? [13]No one has ascended into heaven but he who descended from heaven, the Son of man.[g] [14]And as Moses lifted up the serpent in the wilderness, so must the Son of man be lifted up, [15]that whoever believes in him may have eternal life."[h]

[d] Greek him
[e] Or from above
[f] The same Greek word means both wind and spirit
[g] Other ancient authorities add who is in heaven
[h] Some interpreters hold that the quotation continues through verse 21

HOWARD NEMEROV

Nicodemus

I

I went under cover of night
By back streets and alleyways,
Not as one secret and ashamed
But with a natural discretion.

I passed by a boy and a girl
Embraced against the white wall
In parts of shadow, parts of light,
But though I turned my eyes away, my mind shook
Whether with dryness or their driving blood;
And a dog howled once in a stone corner.

II

Rabbi, I said,
How is a man born, being old?
From the torn sea into the world
A man may be forced only the one time
To suffer the indignation of the child,
His childish distempers and illnesses.
I would not, if I could, be born again
To suffer the miseries of the child,
The perpetual nearness to tears,
The book studied through burning eyes,
The particular malady of being always ruled
To ends he does not see or understand.

A man may be forced only the one time
To the slow perception of what is meant
That is neither final nor sufficient,
To the slow establishment of a self
Adequate to the ceremony and respect
Of other men's eyes; and to the last
Knowledge that nothing has been done,
The bitter bewilderment of his age,
A master in Israel and still a child.

III

Rabbi, all things in the springtime
Flower again, but a man may not
Flower again. I regret
The sweet smell of lilacs and the new grass
And the shoots put forth of the cedar
When we are done with the long winter.

Rabbi, sorrow has mothered me
And humiliation been my father,
But neither the ways of the flesh
Nor the pride of the spirit took me,
And I am exalted in Israel
For all that I know I do not know.

Now the end of my desire is death
For my hour is almost come.
I shall not say with Sarah
That God hath made me to laugh,
Nor the new word shall not be born
Out of the dryness of my mouth.

Rabbi, let me go up from Egypt
With Moses to the wilderness of Sinai
And to the country of the old Canaan
Where, sweeter than honey, Sarah's blood
Darkens the cold cave in the field
And the wild seed of Abraham is cold.

CALLING THE DISCIPLES

LUKE 5:1–11
(Parallel texts: Matthew 4:18–22; Mark 1:16–20)

5 While the people pressed upon him to hear the word of God, he was standing by the lake of Gennes'aret. ²And he saw two boats by the lake; but the fishermen had gone out of them and were washing their nets. ³Getting into one of the boats, which was Simon's, he asked him to put out a little from the land. And he sat down and taught the people from the boat. ⁴And when he had ceased speaking, he said to Simon, "Put out into the deep and let down your nets for a catch." ⁵And Simon answered, "Master, we toiled all night and took nothing! But at your word I will let down the nets." ⁶And when they had done this, they enclosed a great shoal of fish; and as their nets were breaking, ⁷they beckoned to their partners in the other boat to come and help them. And they came and filled both the boats, so that they began to sink. ⁸But when Simon Peter saw it, he fell down at Jesus' knees, saying, "Depart from me, for I am a sinful man, O Lord." ⁹For he was astonished, and all that were with him, at the catch of fish which they had taken; ¹⁰and so also were James and John, sons of Zeb'edee, who were partners with Simon. And Jesus said to Simon, "Do not be afraid; henceforth you will be catching men." ¹¹And when they had brought their boats to land, they left everything and followed him.

CZESLAW MILOSZ

Abundant Catch (Luke 5:4–10)

On the shore fish toss in the stretched nets of Simon, James, and
    John.
High above, swallows. Wings of butterflies. Cathedrals.

Translated from the Polish
by Czeslaw Milosz and Lillian Vallee

THE SERMON ON THE MOUNT

MATTHEW 5:1–12
(Parallel text: Luke 6:20–23)

5 Seeing the crowds, he went up on the mountain, and when he sat down his disciples came to him. ²And he opened his mouth and taught them, saying:

3 "Blessed are the poor in spirit, for theirs is the kingdom of heaven.

4 "Blessed are those who mourn, for they shall be comforted,

5 "Blessed are the meek, for they shall inherit the earth.

6 "Blessed are those who hunger and thirst for righteousness, for they shall be satisfied.

7 "Blessed are the merciful, for they shall obtain mercy.

8 "Blessed are the pure in heart, for they shall see God.

9 "Blessed are the peacemakers, for they shall be called sons of God.

10 "Blessed are those who are persecuted for righteousness' sake, for theirs is the kingdom of heaven.

11 "Blessed are you when men revile you and persecute you and utter all kinds of evil against you falsely on my account. ¹²Rejoice and be glad, for your reward is great in heaven, for so men persecuted the prophets who were before you."

3: *Poor in spirit,* Is.66.2.
5: Ps.37.11.
6: Is.55.1–2.
8: Purity of *heart,* Ps.24.4.
12: 2 Chr.36.15–16.

JORGE LUIS BORGES

From an Apocryphal Gospel

3 Wretched are the poor in spirit: for what they were on earth, so shall they be in their graves.

4 Wretched are they that mourn: for theirs is the cowardly habit of tears.

5 Blessed are they which wear not their suffering as a crown of glory.

6 It availeth not to be the last so as one day to be the first.

7 Blessed is he who insisteth not in being in the right: for no man is wholly in the right.

8 Blessed is he who forgiveth others, and he who forgiveth himself.

9 Blessed are the meek: for they stoop not to the conflict.

10 Blessed are they which hunger not after righteousness: for they see that our lot, whether kindly or cruel, is an act of chance and unknowable.

11 Blessed are the merciful: for their happiness is in showing mercy, not in obtaining reward.

12 Blessed are the pure in heart: for they already see God.

13 Blessed are they which are persecuted for righteousness' sake: for righteousness counteth more to them than they themselves.

14 No man is the salt of the earth: but no man in some moment of his life hath not been the salt of the earth.

15 Let a candle be lighted, though no man see it. God will see it.

16 There is no commandment which may not be broken: neither those I say unto you, nor those laid down by the prophets.

17 Whosoever shall kill for righteousness' sake, or for the sake of what he believeth righteous, he shall bear no guilt.

18 The deeds of men are worthy neither of heaven nor hell.

19 Hate not thine enemy: for if thou cursest him, thou art in some measure his slave: for thy hatred shall never comfort thee as thy peace.

20 And if thy right hand offend thee, forgive it: for thou art thy whole body and thy whole soul, and it is not profitable for thee to divide them. . . .

24 Thou shalt not magnify the worship of truth: for at the day's end there is no man who hath not lied many times with good reason.

25 Neither shalt thou swear, because an oath may be no more than an emphasis.

26 Resist evil: but without either wonder or wrath. Whosoever shall smite thee on thy right cheek, turn to him the other also, so long as thou be not moved by fear.

27 I speak neither of avenging nor forgiving: for the only vengeance and the only forgiveness is forgetting.

28 To bless thine enemy may be righteous and is not difficult: but to love him is a task for angels, not for men.

29 To bless thine enemy is a good way to satisfy thy vanity.

30 Lay not up for thyself treasures upon earth: for treasure is the father of idleness, and idleness of boredom and woe.

31 Look on others as righteous, or as capable of righteousness: for if they are not, the fault is not thine.

32 God is more generous than men, and he will measure them by another measure.

33 Give that which is holy unto the dogs, cast thy pearls before swine: for the thing that mattereth is giving.

34 Seek for the pleasure of seeking, and not for the pleasure of finding. . . .

39 It is the gate that chooseth, and not the man.

40 Judge not the tree by its fruits, nor the man by his works: for the tree and the man may be better or worse.

41 Nothing is built upon rock: for all is built upon sand: but let each man build as if sand were rock. . . .

47 Happy is the poor man without bitterness, and the rich man without arrogance.

48 Happy are the valiant, who in one and the same spirit accept laurel or ash.

49 Happy are they that keep in their memory the words of Virgil or Christ: for these words shall shed light on men's days.

50 Happy are the lovers and the loved, and they that can do without love.

51 Happy are the happy.

Translated from the Spanish
by Norman Thomas di Giovanni

NICANOR PARRA

from *New Sermons and Preachings of the Christ of Elqui (1979)*

XXXII

Who are my friends
the sick
    the weak
        the poor in spirit
those with no place to fall down dead
the old people
    the children
        the unwed mothers
—not students because they're rebellious—
country people because they're humble

fishermen
          because they remind me
of the apostles of Christ
those who never knew their fathers
those who lost their mother as I did
those sentenced to life in prison
in so-called government offices
those humiliated by their own children
those insulted by their wives
the Araucanians*
those who are passed over time after time
those who can't write their names
the bakers   the gravediggers
those are my friends
the dreamers
          the idealists
who sacrificed their lives
as He did for a better world.

Translated from the Spanish
by Sandra Reyes

*An Indian tribe also known as the Mapuche, who live mainly in southern Chile.

BRUCE DAWE

Beatitudes

Blessed are the files marked ACTION in the INWARD tray,
    for they shall be actioned;
Blessed are the memos from above stamped forthrightly
    in magenta FOR IMMEDIATE ATTENTION
        for they shall receive it;
Blessed are the telephones that chirrup and the marvellous
    conundrums conveyed thereby;
Blessed also the intercom calling this one or that from
    his labours that he may enter into the Presence;
Blessed the air-conditioning system bringing a single guaranteed
    hygienic weather within these walls;
Blessed the discreet articulation of management
    by whose leave the heart beats;
Blessed the barbiturate of years, the desk-calendar's inexorable
    snow, the farewells rippling the typing-pool's
        serenity, the Christmas Eve parties where men choke quietly
                over
        the unaccustomed cigar and the elderly file-clerks
           squeal at the shy randyness of their seniors;
Blessed the punch-card fantasies of the neat young men
    whom only the blotter's doodling betrays;
Blessed the complete liturgy of longing, the stubbed grief,
    the gulped joy, the straightened seams, the Glo-weave yes,
        the rubberized love, the shined air, the insensible clouds,
        the dream rain and see there over and above
           the rainbow's wrecked girders
              the pterodactyl smile . . .

ANNA KAMIENSKA

Those Who Carry

Those who carry grand pianos
to the tenth floor   wardrobes and coffins
the old man with a bundle of wood hobbling beyond the horizon
the woman with a hump of nettles
the lunatic pushing her baby carriage
full of empty vodka bottles
they all will be raised up
like a seagull feather   like a dry leaf
like eggshell   scraps of street newspapers

Blessed are those who carry
for they will be raised

Translated from the Polish
by David Curzon and Grażyna Drabik

TOM DISCH

The Garage Sale as a Spiritual Exercise

Once someone loved this piece of junk
If only for a moment at the mall
With its wrappings intact
And its price so much reduced.
You need me, it whispered,
And he couldn't disagree.
So he bought it, the way he bought
Everything he'd ever been sold,
In the belief that it would do the job.
And it did, for the longest time,
And never broke down or wore out
And in fact has outlasted him,
Because here it is, a sickly blue,
In the basement of the Methodist Church,
And now it means to have you.
You sneer at it and think: No way.
You can see only its tackiness,
The virus invisible back at the mall
Which now blots out all its viable features
Like triumphant acne. You don't see
The years of loving drudgery,
The promises fulfilled.
It needs you now, don't turn away.
Take it to the lady and ask what it costs.
Don't be proud. Remember the Beatitudes
And who gets the kingdom of heaven.

MATTHEW 5:13
(Parallel texts: Mark 9:50; Luke 14:34)

13 "You are the salt of the earth; but if salt has lost its taste, how shall its saltness be restored? It is no longer good for anything except to be thrown out and trodden under foot by men.["]

MATTHEW 5:27–30

27 "You have heard that it was said, 'You shall not commit adultery.' [28]But I say to you that every one who looks at a woman lustfully has already committed adultery with her in his heart. [29]If your right eye causes you to sin, pluck it out and throw it away; it is better that you lose one of your members than that your whole body be thrown into hell.[k] [30]And if your right hand causes you to sin, cut it off and throw it away; it is better that you lose one of your members than that your whole body go into hell.[k]["]

[k] Greek *Gehenna*

27: Ex.20.14; Dt.5.18.

GAIL HOLST-WARHAFT

The Old Men of Athens

The old men's wives
are the salt of the earth,
bitterly waiting
for their men to return
from the tavern where
they sing and dream.

When the old men dance
their steps are small
and light as air.
For a moment they tread
the savourless salt
of every day
under their feet
until the bouzouki
stops, and their
worn overcoats
slumped on chair-backs
remind them of
the salt of the earth.

A. D. HOPE

Gloss to Matthew V 27–28

What wisdom and beauty his Sermon on the Mount
Displays, what energy and prophetic fire!
Yet one phrase, for which I still cannot account,
Reveals the innocence of the young Messiah.

"Thou shalt not commit adultery!" We concur
In what was said of old. Now hear the harder part:
"He who looks on a woman to lust after her,
Has committed adultery already in his heart."

I have often pondered, and I ponder still
That astonishing statement which condemns desire.
Did he think it possible by a mere act of will
To ward off lightning, douse unquenchable fire?

Was it easier for a son of God to smother
Thoughts innate to the rest of humankind?
Or did perhaps, having a virgin mother
Endow him, rather, with a virgin mind?

He was not prurient; he was no puritan;
His mind was generous as the gospel records.
He called himself Son of God, but also Son of Man:
Which of his two natures spoke those daunting words?

Their inhumanity is what makes them odd.
I hold with Blake: "The nakedness of woman
Is the glory of God!" I answer the Son of God:
Adultery in the heart proclaims me human.

When she moves in her beauty, the heart responds unbidden.
Too late then to deny involuntary delight.
And surely he knew how things suppressed and hidden
Infect us with dreams to dupe us in the night.

He spoke, some will say, not of rational admiration
But of animal passion. To take these feelings apart
I offer them Occam's razor for their operation
Of excluding Love from Adultery in the Heart.

It cannot be done. Each interfuses the other,
Partakes of the other's nature as water mingles with wine.
To condemn desire is to deny and smother
The root of love. But I take a harder line.

Against that phrase, whose sense, I am afraid,
Duly considered borders on the obscene,
I invoke Peter's dream: "What God has made
Call not thou common or unclean!"

MATTHEW 5:38–48
(Parallel text: Luke 6:27–36)

38 "You have heard that it was said, 'An eye for an eye and a tooth for a tooth.' ³⁹But I say to you, Do not resist one who is evil. But if any one strikes you on the right cheek, turn to him the other also; ⁴⁰and if any one would sue you and take your coat, let him have your cloak as well; ⁴¹and if any one forces you to go one mile, go with him two miles. ⁴²Give to him who begs from you, and do not refuse him who would borrow from you.

43 "You have heard that it was said, 'You shall love your neighbor and hate your enemy.' ⁴⁴But I say to you, Love your enemies and pray for those who persecute you, ⁴⁵so that you may be sons of your Father who is in heaven; for he makes his sun rise on the evil and on the good, and sends rain on the just and on the unjust. ⁴⁶For if you love those who love you, what reward have you? Do not even the tax collectors do the same? ⁴⁷And if you salute only your brethren, what more are you doing than others? Do not even the Gentiles do the same? ⁴⁸You, therefore, must be perfect, as your heavenly Father is perfect.["]

38: Ex.21.23–24; Lev.24.19–20; Dt.19.21.

JACOB GLATSTEIN

How Much Christian*

How much Christian, so to speak, can I get?
How much pity was left me
And what can I forgive?
Maybe I can throw a few soft crumbs
On the account of one tiny life.
But what about the divine annihilation?
Do I have any permission from them?
Who am I to betray
The Burning Bush of death?

All my face-slappers have slapped both my cheeks.
Cossacks have never given a Mishnah-Jew
A chance to turn his other cheek.
How much Jew can I convert in myself, so to speak?
A pinch. So much pity
They can still get out of me
For the children of my leprous enemies.
This pinch of sympathy—take it from me, toss.
But do not shadow my heart
With a pitiful cross.

Translated from the Yiddish
by Benjamin Harshav and Barbara Harshav

*A note on this poem can be found on page 268.

D. H. LAWRENCE

Commandments

When Jesus commanded us to love our neighbour
he forced us either to live a great lie, or to disobey:
for we can't love anybody, neighbour or no neighbour, to order,
and faked love has rotted our marrow.

YUSEF IMAN

Love Your Enemy

Brought here in slave ships and pitched overboard
Love your enemy
Language taken away, culture taken away
Love your enemy
Work from sun up to sun down
Love your enemy
Last hired, first fired
Love your enemy
Rape your mother
Love your enemy
Lynch your father
Love your enemy
Bomb your churches
Love your enemy
Kill your children
Love your enemy
Forced to fight his Wars
Love your enemy
Pay the highest rent
Love your enemy
Sell you rotten food
Love your enemy
Forced to live in the slums
Love your enemy
Dilapidated schools
Love your enemy
Puts you in jail
Love your enemy

Bitten by dogs
Love your enemy
Water hose you down
Love your enemy
Love,
Love,
Love,
Love,
Love, for everybody else,
     but when will we love ourselves?

LEONID ZAVALNIUK

I Love My Enemies

I love my enemies, those I forgive;
they are my friends.
But at times, when fate lies like a stone,
there is a dying in my soul,
and I'm prepared to love even those
no one should forgive,
just because life is hard work.
Any life. Any at all.

. . . You burned down my house
so you could warm yourself by the fire.
You trampled my hopes.
Who can measure my loss?
Still, I'm grateful, friend:
you didn't kill me,
though you're stronger than I am
and don't believe in anything at all.

Translated from the Russian
by Magda Bogin

VAHAN TEKEYAN

Sacred Wrath

The patience of the lambs was exhausted.
Even the time to remain lamb must terminate.
The sacrificial doves before the altar
fluttered up dissatisfied with fate.

The lilies of the field revolted,
cringing from their dignified, clean stance.
The violets in the dark moss decided
to exhale only acrid fragrance then.

The lambs transformed to wolves, doves to snakes,
saw lilies become thistles and
violets change to poison vine and root.

Indignant, just, ancient saints rebelled
crying: Enough of kissing the executioner's hand.
It is our turn to execute.

1903

Translated from the Armenian
by Diana Der-Hovanessian and Marsbed Margossian

TED HUGHES

Crow's Theology

Crow realized God loved him—
Otherwise, he would have dropped dead.
So that was proved.
Crow reclined, marvelling, on his heart-beat.

And he realized that God spoke Crow—
Just existing was His revelation.

But what
Loved the stones and spoke stone?
They seemed to exist too.
And what spoke that strange silence
After his clamour of caws faded?

And what loved the shot-pellets
That dribbled from those strung-up mummifying crows?
What spoke the silence of lead?

Crow realized there were two Gods—

One of them much bigger than the other
Loving his enemies
And having all the weapons.

MATTHEW 6:7–15
(Parallel text: Luke 11:2–4)

7 "And in praying do not heap up empty phrases as the Gentiles do; for they think that they will be heard for their many words. ⁸Do not be like them, for your Father knows what you need before you ask him. ⁹Pray then like this:

Our Father who art in heaven,
Hallowed be thy name.
¹⁰Thy kingdom come.
  Thy will be done,
    On earth as it is in heaven.
¹¹Give us this day our daily bread;ᵐ
¹²And forgive us our debts,
    As we also have forgiven our debtors;
¹³And lead us not into temptation,
    But deliver us from evil.ⁿ
¹⁴For if you forgive men their trespasses, your heavenly Father also will forgive you; ¹⁵but if you do not forgive men their trespasses, neither will your Father forgive your trespasses.["]

ᵐ Or *our bread for the morrow*
ⁿ Or *the evil one.* Other authorities, some ancient, add, in some form, *For thine is the kingdom and the power and the glory, for ever. Amen.*
On the basis of David's prayer (1 Chr.29.11–13) the early church added an appropriate concluding doxology (see note *n*).

9: Is.63.16; 64.8.

D. H. LAWRENCE

Lord's Prayer

For thine is the kingdom
the power, and the glory—

Hallowed be thy name, then
Thou who art nameless—

Give me, Oh give me
besides my daily bread
my kingdom, my power, and my glory.

All things that turn to thee
have their kingdom, their power, and their glory.

Like the kingdom of the nightingale at twilight
whose power and glory I have often heard and felt.

Like the kingdom of the fox in the dark
yapping in his power and his glory
which is death to the goose.

Like the power and the glory of the goose in the mist
honking over the lake.

And I, a naked man, calling
calling to thee for my mana,
my kingdom, my power, and my glory.

JACQUES PRÉVERT

Our Father

Our Father who art in heaven
Stay there
And we'll stay here on earth
Which is so pretty sometimes
With her New York mysteries
And also her Paris mysteries
Easily worth those of the Trinity
With her little canal at Ourq
Her Great Wall of China
Her river of Morlaix
Her after-dinner mints from Cambrai
Her Pacific Ocean
And two ponds in the Tuileries
With her good children and bad subjects
With all the marvels of the world
Which are there
Simply on the earth
Offered to everyone
Scattered
Themselves marvelling at being such marvels
That dare not admit it
Like a pretty girl who dares not show herself naked
With the terrible disasters of the world
Which are legion
With their legionnaires
With their torturers
With the masters of this world
The masters with their priests their traitors their thugs
With the seasons
The years
The pretty girls and the old fools
With the straw of misery rotting in the steel of cannons.

Translated from the French by Jeffrey Fiskin

NICANOR PARRA

Lord's Prayer

Our Father which art in heaven
Full of all manner of problems
With a wrinkled brow
(As if you were a common everyday man)
Think no more of us.

We understand that you suffer
Because you can't put everything in order.

We know the Demon will not leave you alone
Tearing down everything you build.

He laughs at you
But we weep with you:
Don't pay any attention to his devilish laughter.

Our Father who art where thou art
Surrounded by unfaithful Angels
Sincerely don't suffer any more for us
You must take into account
That the gods are not infallible
And that we have come to forgive everything.

Translated from the Spanish
by Miller Williams

ANTONIO MACHADO

Lord, You Have Ripped Away

Lord, you have ripped away from me what I loved most.
One more time, O God, hear me cry out inside.
"Your will be done," it was done, and mine not.
My heart and the sea are together, Lord, and alone.

Translated from the Spanish
by Robert Bly

CÉSAR VALLEJO

Our Daily Bread

(for Alejandro Gamboa)

Breakfast is drunk down . . . Damp earth
of the cemetery gives off the fragrance of the precious blood.
City of winter . . . the mordant crusade
of a cart that seems to pull behind it
an emotion of fasting that cannot get free!

I wish I could beat on all the doors,
and ask for somebody; and then
look at the poor, and, while they wept softly,
give bits of fresh bread to them.
And plunder the rich of their vineyards
with those two blessed hands
which blasted the nails with one blow of light,
and flew away from the Cross!

Eyelash of morning, you cannot lift yourselves!
Give us our daily bread,
Lord . . . !

Every bone in me belongs to others;
and maybe I robbed them.
I came to take something for myself that maybe
was meant for some other man;
and I start thinking that, if I had not been born,
another poor man could have drunk this coffee.
I feel like a dirty thief . . . Where will I end?

And in this frigid hour, when the earth
has the odor of human dust and is so sad,
I wish I could beat on all the doors
and beg pardon from someone,
and make bits of fresh bread for him
here, in the oven of my heart . . . !

Translated from the Spanish
by James Wright

ERIC PANKEY

As We Forgive Those

You're excused, my father would say.
                                    My father
was last to get up from the dinner table.
When I heard the word I heard its rhyme *accused.*
All my life I was a child. I waited
for someone to say my name. I stood in lines.
I learned to forgive from those who forgave me.
I can't remember now if I was supposed
to forgive those who trespassed, or my debtors.
Trespass was what I did for apples, for fun.
I stole green tomatoes and dropped them from trees.
I crouched behind low junipers, waited,
my bare knees on the brown dried prickers, bagworms
hanging as thick as the hard blue berries, waited
for a glimpse of someone naked, a crime,
something only I would see and know.
                                    That year
in school I learned the word *omniscient.*
I learned other words as well, but what I loved
were the words that no one would ever use.
We always owed someone or someone owed us
and that's why we didn't talk about money.
I don't think we ever used the word *debtor.*
Give us this day we would say in that prayer
as if the day were not already ours.
When I'd come home and find my parents yelling,
they would tell me not to worry; it didn't
concern me.
                    That's what I thought forgiveness was.
Being excused from something you knew nothing
about. Sometimes I'd wake and hear them talking,
kindly, intimately, with the care one takes

when a baby is asleep in the same room.
Those were nights I'd pray, nights I'd talk aloud
so I wouldn't have to listen to my heart
go about its business.
                              I prayed for knowledge,
although those nights I couldn't have called it that.
I knew there'd be something for which I'd be blamed.
I knew someday I'd stumble unknowingly,
if I hadn't already. I knew enough
to pray for something possible. I said *Give us*
this day and when the night passed the day was there.
I walked out beneath the maple that ruled
our house half the day in sunlight, half in shade.
Its shadow swept every inch of what we owned.
When it covered me I knew I was forgiven.

ANNE WINTERS

The Mill-Race

Four-fifty. The palings of Trinity Church
Burying Ground, a few inches above the earth,
are sunk in green light. The low stones
like pale books knocked sideways. The bus so close to the curb
that brush-drops of ebony paint stand out wetly, the sunlight
seethes with vibrations, the sidewalks
on Whitehall shudder with subterranean tremors. Overhead, faint
      flickers

crackle down the window-paths: limpid telegraphy of the
late afternoon July thunderstorm unfurling over Manhattan.
Its set and luminous velocity, the long stalks of stormlight, and
      then the first drops
strike their light civic stripes on the pavement.
Between the palings, oat-panicles sift a few bright
grains to the stonecourse. Above it, at shoulder height,
a side door is flung open; a fire-exit; streaming from lobbies

come girls and women, black girls with ripples of cornrows and
      plaits,
ear-hoops, striped shadowy cotton-topped skirts, white girls in
      gauzy-toned nylons,
one girl with shocked-back ash hair, lightened eyebrows;
one face from Easter Island, mauve and granitic;
thigh on thigh, waist by waist; the elbow's curlicue and the
      fingers'; elbow-work, heel-work,
are suddenly absorbed in the corduroyed black-rubber stairs of
      the bus. Humid
sighs, settlings, each face tilts up to the windows'
shadowless yards of mercuric green plateglass. In close-up

you can see it in the set and grain of each face,
despite the roped rainlight pouring in the bus-windows—
it's the strain of gravity itself, life-hours cut off and offered
to the voice that says, "Give me this day your
life, that is LABOR, and I'll give you back
one day, then another. For mine are the terms."
It's gravity, spilling in capillaries, cheek-tissue trembling
despite the makeup, the monograms, the mass-market designer
    scarves,
the army of private signs disowning the workplace and longing
    for night. . . .

But this, at least, is the interspace. Like the slowing of some rural
water mill, a creaking and dipping pause
of black-splintered paddles, the irregularly
dappled off-lighting—bottle-green—the lucid slim sluice
falling back in a spittle-stream from the plank-edge. It won't take
    us
altogether, we say, the mill-race—it won't churn us up,
    altogether. We'll keep
this glib stretch of leisure-water, like our self's self—to reflect the
    sky.
But we won't (says the bus-rider, slumped, to herself). Nothing's
left over, really, from labor. They've taken it all for the mill-race.
    Even now,

as the driver flicks off the huge felt-edged wipers,
the rain slackening, lifting, labor
lengthens itself along Broadway. Fresh puddles
mirror in amber and crimson the night signs
that wit has set up to draw money: O'Donnell's,
Beirut Café, Yonah's Knish . . . People dart out from awnings.
The old man at the kiosk starts his late shift, whipping off rain-
    streaked
Lucite sheets from his new stacks of newsprint.

If there is leisure, bus-riders, it's not for you,
not between here and uptown or here and the Bronx. . . .
Outside Marine Midland, the black sea of unmarked corporate
    hire-cars
waits for the belated office-lights, the long rainy run to the
    exurbs.
Somewhere it may be, on a converted barn-roof in Connecticut,
leisure silvers the shingles, somewhere the densely packed
labor-mines running a half-mile down from the sky
to the Battery's bedrock rise, metamorphic, in water-gardens,
lichened windows where the lamp lights Thucydides or Gibbon.

It's not a water mill really, work. It's like the nocturnal
paper-mill pulverizing, crushing each fiber of rag into atoms,
or the smooth-lipped workhouse
treadmill, that wore down a London of doxies and sharps,
or the paper-mill, faërique, that raised the cathedrals and wore
    out hosts of dust-demons,
but it's mostly the miller's curse-gift, forgotten of God yet still
    grinding, the salt-
mill, that makes the sea, salt.

STANISŁAW BARAŃCZAK

N. N. Tries to Remember the Words of a Prayer

Our Father, who art speechless,
who art deaf to every plea,
and lets us know the world is still turning
only by the daily braying of factory sirens,
speak to us:
that girl taking the tram to work,
in the cheap raincoat, with three rings

on her fingers, with sleep still tugging at her eyelids,
must hear Your voice,
must hear Your voice, if she's to wake
for yet another day.

Our Father, who art unknowing,
who dost not even look down at this earth,
but merely announces in the daily papers that the world,
our world,
is still in order, look down:
the man at that table, bent over his rissole, his glass of vodka,
his evening paper thick with gravy and newsprint,
must know that You also know,
must know You know, if he's to live
through yet another day.

Our Father, who art not,
whose name is never even invoked
except in didactic booklets that print it in lower case,
because the world
goes on without You,
come into being:
the man who goes to bed counting
all his lies, fears, and treacheries of the day,
all those inevitable and fully justifiable acts of shame,
must believe You do exist,
must believe You exist, if he's to sleep
through yet another night.

Translated from the Polish
by Kevin Windle

MATTHEW 7:1–2
(Parallel text: Luke 6:37–38)

7 "Judge not, that you be not judged. ²For with the judgment you pronounce you will be judged, and the measure you give will be the measure you get.["]

THEODORE ROETHKE

Judge Not

Faces greying faster than loam-crumbs on a harrow;
Children, their bellies swollen like blown-up paper bags,
Their eyes rich as plums, staring from newsprint,—
These images haunted me noon and midnight.
I imagined the unborn, starving in wombs, curling;
I asked: May the blessings of life, O Lord, descend on the living.

Yet when I heard the drunkards howling,
Smelled the carrion at entrances,
Saw women, their eyelids like little rags,
I said: On all these, Death, with gentleness, come down.

THE BIRDS OF THE AIR

MATTHEW 8:20

20 And Jesus said to him, "Foxes have holes, and birds of the air have nests; but the Son of man has nowhere to lay his head."

KARL KIRCHWEY

He Considers the Birds of the Air

(MATTHEW 8:20)

We get up at six with him and build a fire.
    Against a choir of straight second-growth woods
    on a morning when the thermometer stands
at zero, he considers the birds of the air.

They hop down and again hop down to the feeder
    beyond the window for the black sunflower seeds
    or the suet's white shoulder, a traffic of chickadees
to which cardinals and pine grosbeaks add color.

His man-in-the-moon face, his eyes of cracked sapphire
    reflect necessity in that repeated
    motion. An infant gazes at some birds,
and for a moment it all balances there,

unblinking, calm, until the slightest feather
    of snow, knocked free by a breeze, drifts toward
    the ground, past curtains hospitably patterned
in red-and-blue chintz pineapples: mute glitter,

crystal fusillade. He will have nowhere
    to lay his head, no matter how he builds,
    no matter how he watches where unnumbered
small creatures have their being in the weather.

THE GADARENE SWINE

MATTHEW 8:28−34
(Parallel texts: Mark 5:1−20; Luke 8:26−39)

28 And when he came to the other side, to the country of the Gadarenes,[1] two demoniacs met him, coming out of the tombs, so fierce that no one could pass that way. [29]And behold, they cried out, "What have you to do with us, O Son of God? Have you come here to torment us before the time?" [30]Now a herd of many swine was feeding at some distance from them. [31]And the demons begged him, "If you cast us out, send us away into the herd of swine." [32]And he said to them, "Go." So they came out and went into the swine; and behold, the whole herd rushed down the steep bank into the sea, and perished in the waters. [33]The herdsmen fled, and going into the city they told everything, and what had happened to the demoniacs. [34]And behold, all the city came out to meet Jesus; and when they saw him, they begged him to leave their neighborhood.

[1] Other ancient authorities read *Gergesenes;* some, *Gerasenes*

RICHARD WILBUR

Matthew VIII, 28 ff.

Rabbi, we Gadarenes
Are not ascetics; we are fond of wealth and possessions.
Love, as you call it, we obviate by means
Of the planned release of aggressions.

We have deep faith in prosperity.
Soon, it is hoped, we will reach our full potential.
In the light of our gross product, the practice of charity
Is palpably inessential.

It is true that we go insane;
That for no good reason we are possessed by devils;
That we suffer, despite the amenities which obtain
At all but the lowest levels.

We shall not, however, resign
Our trust in the high-heaped table and the full trough.
If you cannot cure us without destroying our swine,
We had rather you shoved off.

ANTHONY HECHT

Pig

In the manger of course were crows and the Child Himself
                    Was like unto a lamb
Who should come in the fulness of time on an ass's back
                    Into Jerusalem

And all things be redeemed—the suckling babe
                    Lie safe in the serpent's home
And the lion eat straw like the ox and roar its love
                    to Mark and to Jerome

And God's Peaceable Kingdom return among them all
                    Save one full of offense
Into which the thousand fiends of a human soul
                    Were cast and driven hence

And the one thus cured gone up into the hills
                    To worship and to pray:
O Swine that takest away our sins
                    That takest away

CZESLAW MILOSZ

Readings

You asked me what is the good of reading the Gospels in Greek.
I answer that it is proper that we move our finger
Along letters more enduring than those carved in stone,
And that, slowly pronouncing each syllable,
We discover the true dignity of speech.
Compelled to be attentive we shall think of that epoch
No more distant than yesterday, though the heads of caesars
On coins are different today. Yet still it is the same eon.
Fear and desire are the same, oil and wine
And bread mean the same. So does the fickleness of the throng
Avid for miracles as in the past. Even mores,
Wedding festivities, drugs, laments for the dead
Only seem to differ. Then, too, for example,
There were plenty of persons whom the text calls
Daimonizomenoi, that is, the demonized
Or, if you prefer, the bedeviled (as for "the possessed"
It's no more than the whim of a dictionary).
Convulsions, foam at the mouth, the gnashing of teeth
Were not considered signs of talent.
The demonized had no access to print and screens,
Rarely engaging in arts and literature.
But the Gospel parable remains in force:
That the spirit mastering them may enter swine,
Which, exasperated by such a sudden clash
Between two natures, theirs and the Luciferic,
Jump into water and drown (which occurs repeatedly).
And thus on every page a persistent reader
Sees twenty centuries as twenty days
In a world which one day will come to its end.

Berkeley, 1969

Translated from the Polish
by Czeslaw Milosz and Lillian Vallee

THE DAUGHTER OF JAIRUS

MARK 5:21–43
(Parallel texts: Matthew 9:18–26; Luke 8:40–56)

21 And when Jesus had crossed again in the boat to the other side, a great crowd gathered about him; and he was beside the sea. ²²Then came one of the rulers of the synagogue, Ja′irus by name; and seeing him, he fell at his feet, ²³and besought him, saying, "My little daughter is at the point of death. Come and lay your hands on her, so that she may be made well, and live." ²⁴And he went with him. . . .

35 While he was still speaking, there came from the ruler's house some who said, "Your daughter is dead. Why trouble the Teacher any further?" ³⁶But ignoring⁴ what they said, Jesus said to the ruler of the synagogue, "Do not fear, only believe." ³⁷And he allowed no one to follow him except Peter and James and John the brother of James. ³⁸When they came to the house of the ruler of the synagogue, he saw a tumult, and people weeping and wailing loudly. ³⁹And when he had entered, he said to them, "Why do you make a tumult and weep? The child is not dead but sleeping." ⁴⁰And they laughed at him. But he put them all outside, and took the child's father and mother and those who were with him, and went in where the child was. ⁴¹Taking her by the hand he said to her, "Tal′itha cu′mi"; which means, "Little girl, I say to you, arise." ⁴²And immediately the girl got up and walked (she was twelve years of age), and they were immediately overcome with amazement. ⁴³And he strictly charged them that no one should know this, and told them to give her something to eat.

---

⁴ Or *overhearing*. Other ancient authorities read *hearing*

41: The phrase *talitha cumi* preserves the actual (as distinct from translated) Aramaic words of Jesus (see 2 Kg.18.26).

CZESLAW MILOSZ

With Her*

Those poor, arthritically swollen knees
Of my mother in an absent country.
I think of them on my seventy-fourth birthday
As I attend early Mass at St. Mary Magdalen in Berkeley.
A reading this Sunday from the Book of Wisdom
About how God had not made death
And does not rejoice in the annihilation of the living.
A reading from the Gospel according to Mark
About a little girl to whom He said: "Talitha, cumi!"
This is for me. To make me rise from the dead
And repeat the hope of those who lived before me,
In a fearful unity with her, with her pain of dying,
In a village near Danzig, in a dark November,
When both the mournful Germans, old men and women,
And the evacuees from Lithuania would fall ill with typhus.
Be with me, I say to her, my time has been short.
Your word are now mine, deep inside me:
"It all seems now to have been a dream."

Berkeley, 1985

Translated from the Polish
by Robert Hass and Czeslaw Milosz

*A note on this poem can be found on page 268.

HEALING THE SICK

MATTHEW 10:1
(Parallel texts: Mark 6:7; Luke 9:1–2)

10 And he called to him his twelve disciples and gave them authority over unclean spirits, to cast them out, and to heal every disease and every infirmity.

PHILIP LARKIN

Faith Healing*

Slowly the women file to where he stands
Upright in rimless glasses, silver hair,
Dark suit, white collar. Stewards tirelessly
Persuade them onwards to his voice and hands,
Within whose warm spring rain of loving care
Each dwells some twenty seconds. Now, dear child,
What's wrong, the deep American voice demands,
And, scarcely pausing, goes into a prayer
Directing God about this eye, that knee.
Their heads are clasped abruptly; then, exiled

Like losing thoughts, they go in silence; some
Sheepishly stray, not back into their lives
Just yet; but some stay stiff, twitching and loud
With deep hoarse tears, as if a kind of dumb
And idiot child within them still survives
To re-awake at kindness, thinking a voice
At last calls them alone, that hands have come
To lift and lighten; and such joy arrives
Their thick tongues blort, their eyes squeeze grief, a crowd
Of huge unheard answers jam and rejoice—

What's wrong! Moustached in flowered frocks they shake:
By now, all's wrong. In everyone there sleeps
A sense of life lived according to love.
To some it means the difference they could make
By loving others, but across most it sweeps
As all they might have done had they been loved.
That nothing cures. An immense slackening ache,
As when, thawing, the rigid landscape weeps,
Spreads slowly through them—that, and the voice above
Saying Dear child, and all time has disproved.

*A note on this poem can be found on page 268.

THE PARABLE OF THE SOWER

MATTHEW 13:1–9
(Parallel texts: Mark 4:1–9; Luke 8:4–8)

13 That same day Jesus went out of the house and sat beside the sea. ²And great crowds gathered about him, so that he got into a boat and sat there; and the whole crowd stood on the beach. ³And he told them many things in parables, saying: "A sower went out to sow. ⁴And as he sowed, some seeds fell along the path, and the birds came and devoured them. ⁵Other seeds fell on rocky ground, where they had not much soil, and immediately they sprang up, since they had no depth of soil, ⁶but when the sun rose they were scorched; and since they had no root they withered away. ⁷Other seeds fell upon thorns, and the thorns grew up and choked them. ⁸Other seeds fell on good soil and brought forth grain, some a hundred-fold, some sixty, some thirty. ⁹He who has ears,ʰ let him hear."

ʰ Other ancient authorities add here and in verse 43 *to hear*

STEPHEN MITCHELL

The Parable of the Sower

A sower went forth to sow. Some of his seeds fell upon stony places. Centuries passed; millennia. And the seeds remained. And the stones crumbled and became good soil, and the seeds brought forth fruit.

"Wait a minute," said one listener. "You can't play fast and loose that way with the natural facts. The seeds would die long before the soil could receive them."

"Why would they die?"

"Because they can't hold out in stony places, for thousands of years."

"But, my dear, what kind of seeds do you think we're talking about?"

DAVID CURZON

Instructions to a Seed

Don't worry. You're in darkness
now, and very small
but you have it in you.
There's nothing to do except

grow. You've got to draw
your only nourishment from
whatever surrounds you.
You can't change location.

If you fell among thorns it's
too bad. You'll be stifled
or die. No one will care—

there are so many seeds
that are also in darkness
with dispositions. Just grow.

THE PARABLE OF THE BLIND

LUKE 6:39
(Parallel text: Matthew 15:14)

39 He also told them a parable: "Can a blind man lead a blind man? Will they not both fall into a pit?["]

WILLIAM CARLOS WILLIAMS

from *"Pictures from Brueghel"*

IX   *The Parable of the Blind*

This horrible but superb painting
the parable of the blind
without a red

in the composition shows a group
of beggars leading
each other diagonally downward

across the canvas
from one side
to stumble finally into a bog

where the picture
and the composition ends back
of which no seeing man

is represented the unshaven
features of the des-
titute with their few

pitiful possessions a basin
to wash in a peasant
cottage is seen and a church spire

the faces are raised
as toward the light
there is no detail extraneous

to the composition one
follows the others stick in
hand triumphant to disaster

THE GOOD SAMARITAN

LUKE 10:25–37

25 And behold, a lawyer stood up to put him to the test, saying, "Teacher, what shall I do to inherit eternal life?" 26He said to him, "What is written in the law? How do you read?" 27And he answered, "You shall love the Lord your God with all your heart, and with all your soul, and with all your strength, and with all your mind; and your neighbor as yourself." 28And he said to him, "You have answered right; do this, and you will live."

29 But he, desiring to justify himself, said to Jesus, "And who is my neighbor?" 30Jesus replied, "A man was going down from Jerusalem to Jericho, and he fell among robbers, who stripped him and beat him, and departed, leaving him half dead. 31Now by chance a priest was going down that road; and when he saw him he passed by on the other side. 32So likewise a Levite, when he came to the place and saw him, passed by on the other side. 33But a Samaritan, as he journeyed, came to where he was; and when he saw him, he had compassion, 34and went to him and bound up his wounds, pouring on oil and wine; then he set him on his own beast and brought him to an inn, and took care of him. 35And the next day he took out two denarii and gave them to the innkeeper, saying, 'Take care of him; and whatever more you spend, I will repay you when I come back.' 36Which of these three, do you think, proved neighbor to the man who fell among the robbers?" 37He said, "The one who showed mercy on him." And Jesus said to him, "Go and do likewise."

10.25–28: Dt.6.4–5 and Lev.19.18.

STEPHEN MITCHELL

The Good Samaritan et Al.

The priest, the Levite, the Samaritan, and the man who fell among thieves meet in heaven to talk over old times. Since heaven has no past or future, they find themselves in the inn on the road to Jericho.

"I felt awful about not helping you," the priest says. "My heart wasn't open enough. But I'm working on it."

"The last time I had stopped to help a wounded man by the roadside," the Levite says, "he beat me and ran off with my wallet. I was afraid."

"It was my good fortune to be in the right place at the right time," the Samaritan says. "I didn't stop to think; the oil and wine poured themselves, the wound bound itself. My only problem came later, dealing with all the praise."

The man who fell among thieves takes another sip of wine. "Charity begins at home," he says. "If I had been kinder to myself, I wouldn't have been in that mess to begin with. But I am very grateful to all three of you. It takes great humility to step aside, for a parable's sake. And without the parable, I would never have been saved."

MARTHA AND MARY

LUKE 10:38–42

38 Now as they went on their way, he entered a village; and a woman named Martha received him into her house. ³⁹And she had a sister called Mary, who sat at the Lord's feet and listened to his teaching. ⁴⁰But Martha was distracted with much serving; and she went to him and said, "Lord, do you not care that my sister has left me to serve alone? Tell her then to help me." ⁴¹But the Lord answered her, "Martha, Martha, you are anxious and troubled about many things; ⁴²one thing is needful.ʲ Mary has chosen the good portion, which shall not be taken away from her."

ʲ Other ancient authorities read *few things are needful, or only one*

ANNA KAMIENSKA

Saint Martha

Scolded like an impolite child
stopped in mid gesture
with a wooden spoon in one hand
while a bowl falls
from the other
hidden in the dimness of the pantry
under a candelabra of spiderwebs
she is ashamed in the glow of the kitchen fire
she covers her dress with a blue apron
a small dark smudge over her breast
she shades her brow with a starched cloth
in the darkness the barrels are praying
patient with the maturing of malt
the oils' truth settles in clay jugs
a tear trembles on a flaxen eyelash
greatly saddened shadows
brightened only by a glimpse of green gaze
humble and apologetic
but disobedient she still continues to serve
heart in a rush of love
even when her wise sister   a poplar
calmly takes out of her hands a warm loaf of bread covered with
     snow

Translated from the Polish
by David Curzon and Grażyna Drabik

GABRIELA MISTRAL

Martha and Mary

They were born together, lived together,
ate together—Martha and Mary.
They closed the same door,
drank from the same well,
were watched by one thicket,
clothed by one light.

Martha's cups and dishes clattered,
her kettles bubbled.
Her chickenyard teemed with roosters,
a whirr of plover and dove.
She bustled to and fro
lost in a cloud of feathers.

Martha cut the air, reigned
over meals and linen,
governed wine press and beehives,
ruled the minute, the hour, the day . . .

A wounded outcry sounded
wherever she came and went.
Dishes, doors, bolts clamored
as to a belled sheep.
But all grew hushed when her sister passed by,
thin keening and Hail Marys.

In a whitewashed corner,
Mary in blue majolica
wove some strange thing in the quiet air
though she never raised her hand.
What was this thing that never finished,
never altered or increased?

One golden-eyed noon
while Martha with ten hands
was busy reshaping old Judea,
without a word or sign, Mary *passed on.*

She merely grew more languid,
her cheeks indrawn;
the mark of her body and spirit
imprinted in the cold lime,
a trembling fern,
a slow stalactite;
no more than a great silence
that no cry or lightning bolt could shatter.

When Martha grew old,
oven and kitchen grew quiet,
the house gained its sleep,
the ladder lay supine;
and falling asleep,
her flesh shriveling from ruddy to ash,
Martha went to crouch
in Mary's corner
where with wonder and silence
her mouth scarcely moved . . .

She asked to go to Mary
and toward her she went, she went
murmuring, "Mary!"—only that,
repeating, "Mary!"
And she called out with such fervor
that, without knowing, she departed,
letting loose the filament of breath
that her breast did not protect.
Now she left, ascending the air;
now she was no longer and did not know it . . .

Translated from the Spanish
by Doris Dana

RUDYARD KIPLING

The Sons of Martha

The Sons of Mary seldom bother, for they have inherited that
good part;
But the Sons of Martha favour their Mother of the careful soul
and the troubled heart.
And because she lost her temper once, and because she was rude
to the Lord her Guest,
Her Sons must wait upon Mary's Sons, world without end,
reprieve, or rest.

It is their care in all the ages to take the buffet and cushion the
shock.
It is their care that the gear engages; it is their care that the
switches lock.
It is their care that the wheels run truly; it is their care to embark
and entrain,
Tally, transport, and deliver duly the Sons of Mary by land and
main.

They say to mountains, "Be ye removed." They say to the lesser
floods, "Be dry."
Under their rods are the rocks reproved—they are not afraid of
that which is high.
Then do the hill-tops shake to the summit—then is the bed of
the deep laid bare,
That the Sons of Mary may overcome it, pleasantly sleeping and
unaware.

They finger death at their gloves' end where they piece and
repiece the living wires.
He rears against the gates they tend: they feed him hungry
behind their fires.
Early at dawn, ere men see clear, they stumble into his terrible stall,
And hale him forth like a haltered steer, and goad and turn him
till evenfall.

To these from birth is Belief forbidden; from these till death is
    Relief afar.
They are concerned with matters hidden—under the earth-line
    their altars are—
The secret fountains to follow up, waters withdrawn to restore to
    the mouth,
And gather the floods as in a cup, and pour them again at a city's
    drouth.

They do not preach that their God will rouse them a little before
    the nuts work loose.
They do not teach that His Pity allows them to drop their job
    when they dam'-well choose.
As in the thronged and the lighted ways, so in the dark and the
    desert they stand,
Wary and watchful all their days that their brethren's days may
    be long in the land.

Raise ye the stone or cleave the wood to make a path more fair or
    flat—
Lo, it is black already with blood some Son of Martha spilled for
    that!
Not as a ladder from earth to Heaven, not as a witness to any
    creed,
But simple service simply given to his own kind in their common
    need.

And the Sons of Mary smile and are blessed—they know the
    Angels are on their side
They know in them is the Grace confessed, and for them are the
    Mercies multiplied.
They sit at the Feet—they hear the Word—they see how truly
    the Promise runs.
They have cast the burden upon the Lord, and—the Lord He lays
    it on Martha's Sons!

THE PRODIGAL SON

LUKE 15:11–19

11 And he said, "There was a man who had two sons; ¹²and the younger of them said to his father, 'Father, give me the share of property that falls to me.' And he divided his living between them. ¹³Not many days later, the younger son gathered all he had and took his journey into a far country, and there he squandered his property in loose living. ¹⁴And when he had spent everything, a great famine arose in that country, and he began to be in want. ¹⁵So he went and joined himself to one of the citizens of that country, who sent him into his fields to feed swine. ¹⁶And he would gladly have fed on" the pods that the swine ate; and no one gave him anything. ¹⁷But when he came to himself he said, 'How many of my father's hired servants have bread enough and to spare, but I perish here with hunger! ¹⁸I will arise and go to my father, and I will say to him, "Father, I have sinned against heaven and before you; ¹⁹I am no longer worthy to be called your son; treat me as one of your hired servants." '["]

" Other ancient authorities read *filled his belly with*

RAINER MARIA RILKE

The Departure of the Prodigal Son*

Now to depart from all this complication
that's ours without it being our own
and like the water in old well springs
reflects a trembling us and ruins the image;
from all of this, that again attaches
to us, like thorns—and, in departing, give
to odds and ends
which you no longer really see
(they were so normal, ordinary)
re-examination: gently, reconciled,
like some beginning, from nearby,
and to divine just how impersonally,
how over everyone the sorrow came
that filled childhood right to the brim—:
and then to still depart, slipping hand out of hand
as if you wrenched the newly healed,
and to depart: where to? to the unknown,
and on into a warm and steadfast land
that will, for all transactions, be behind
as an indifferent backdrop—garden, wall;
and to depart: but why? from impulse, character,
impatience, vague anticipation,
from not perceiving and the unperceived:

And to absorb all this and then,
perhaps, to needlessly give up,
and die alone not knowing why—

Is this the entry into a new life?

Translated from the German
by David Curzon, Lori Seibel, and Will Alexander Washburn

*A note on this poem can be found on page 268.

W. S. MERWIN

from "*The Prodigal Son*"

for Leueen MacGrath Kaufman

II

And the silence off on the hills might be an echo
Of the silence here in the shadow of the white wall
Where the old man sits brooding upon distance
Upon emptiness. His house behind him,
The white roofs flat and domed, hushed with the heat
And the hour, and making what it can of shadow
While no one stirs, is it in fact the same
In which lifelong he has believed and filled
With life, almost as a larger body, or is it,
Now suddenly in this moment between mirage
And afternoon, another, and farther off
Than the herdsmen, oh much farther, its walls glaring
White out of a different distance, deceiving
By seeming familiar, but an image merely
By which he may know the face of emptiness,
A name with which to say emptiness? Yet it is the same
Where he performs as ever the day's labour,
The gestures of pleasure, as is necessary,
Speaks in the name of order, and is obeyed
Among his sons, except one, except the one
Who took his portion and went. There is no distance
Between himself now and emptiness; he has followed
The departing image of a son beyond
Distance into emptiness. The flies crawl
Unnoticed over his face, through his drooping
Beard, along his hands lying loose as his beard,
Lying in his lap like drying leaves; and before him
The smeared stalls of the beasts, the hens in the shade,
The water-crane still at the well-head, the parched
Fields that are his as far as the herdsmen
Are emptiness in his vacant eyes.

ELIZABETH BISHOP

*The Prodigal**

The brown enormous odor he lived by
was too close, with its breathing and thick hair,
for him to judge. The floor was rotten; the sty
was plastered halfway up with glass-smooth dung.
Light-lashed, self-righteous, above moving snouts,
the pigs' eyes followed him, a cheerful stare—
even to the sow that always ate her young—
till, sickening, he leaned to scratch her head.
But sometimes mornings after drinking bouts
(he hid the pints behind a two-by-four),
the sunrise glazed the barnyard mud with red;
the burning puddles seemed to reassure.
And then he thought he almost might endure
his exile yet another year or more.

But evenings the first star came to warn.
The farmer whom he worked for came at dark
to shut the cows and horses in the barn
beneath their overhanging clouds of hay,
with pitchforks, faint forked lightnings, catching light,
safe and companionable as in the Ark.
The pigs stuck out their little feet and snored.
The lantern—like the sun, going away—
laid on the mud a pacing aureole.
Carrying a bucket along a slimy board,
he felt the bats' uncertain staggering flight,
his shuddering insights, beyond his control,
touching him. But it took him a long time
finally to make his mind up to go home.

*A note on this poem can be found on page 269.

["]²⁰ And he arose and came to his father. But while he was yet at a distance, his father saw him and had compassion, and ran and embraced him and kissed him. ²¹And the son said to him, 'Father, I have sinned against heaven and before you; I am no longer worthy to be called your son.'ᵛ ²²But the father said to his servants, 'Bring quickly the best robe, and put it on him; and put a ring on his hand, and shoes on his feet; ²³and bring the fatted calf and kill it, and let us eat and make merry; ²⁴for this my son was dead, and is alive again; he was lost, and is found.' And they began to make merry.

25 "Now his elder son was in the field; and as he came and drew near to the house, he heard music and dancing. ²⁶And he called one of the servants and asked what this meant. ²⁷And he said to him, 'Your brother has come, and your father has killed the fatted calf, because he has received him safe and sound.' ²⁸But he was angry and refused to go in. His father came out and entreated him, ²⁹but he answered his father, 'Lo, these many years I have served you, and I never disobeyed your command; yet you never gave me a kid, that I might make merry with my friends. ³⁰But when this son of yours came, who has devoured your living with harlots, you killed for him the fatted calf!' ³¹And he said to him, 'Son, you are always with me, and all that is mine is yours. ³²It was fitting to make merry and be glad, for this your brother was dead, and is alive; he was lost, and is found.' "

ᵛ Other ancient authorities add *treat me as one of your hired servants*

EDWIN ARLINGTON ROBINSON

The Prodigal Son

You are not merry, brother. Why not laugh,
As I do, and acclaim the fatted calf?
For, unless ways are changing here at home,
You might not have it if I had not come.
And were I not a thing for you and me
To execrate in anguish, you would be
As indigent a stranger to surprise,
I fear, as I was once, and as unwise.
Brother, believe, as I do, it is best
For you that I'm again in the old nest—
Draggled, I grant you, but your brother still,
Full of good wine, good viands, and good will.
You will thank God, some day, that I returned,
And may be singing for what you have learned,
Some other day; and one day you may find
Yourself a little nearer to mankind.
And having hated me till you are tired
You will begin to see, as if inspired,
It was fate's way of educating us.
Remembering then when you were venomous,
You will be glad enough that I am gone,
But you will know more of what's going on;
For you will see more of what makes it go,
And in more ways than are for you to know.
We are so different when we are dead,
That you, alive, may weep for what you said;
And I, the ghost of one you could not save,
May find you planting lentils on my grave.

LEAH GOLDBERG

The Prodigal Son

I *On the Road*

And the stone on the roadside said then,
"How heavy your steps have grown."
And the stone said, "Will you return now
To your forgotten home?"

And the bush on the roadside said then,
"Your tallness is bent low.
How," said the bush, "will you get there,
Stumbling as you go?"

And the sign-post by the roadside
Cried "Stranger!" in its scorn;
And the sign-post by the roadside
Stabbed him like a thorn.

"Your lips are dry," cried the fountain,
And called from the roadside near.
And he knelt and drank of the water,
And a tear touched a tear.

II *In the House*

"I have forgotten," the sister said.
The brother said, "I do not recall."
"I'll never forgive," the father said.
The bride said, "I've forgiven all."
Silent the mother peeped through the blinds:
Long is the road and far it winds.

"The wind is rising," the sister said.
The brother said, "O hear the rain."
"Locked is the door," the young bride said.
"None," said the father, "shall unlock it again."
Silent the mother walked to and fro:
God in heaven, how cold the winds blow.

"There are five of us," the sister said.
The brother said, "Let us sit and dine."
"Come," said the bride, "the table is laid."
The father said, "I shall pour the wine."
Silent the mother bowed her head,
In five parts broke the Sabbath bread.

The sister nibbled her crumbs like a mouse,
The brother sopped his bread, the bride
Toasted the mistress of the house,
The father ate his bread and sighed.
Then up rose the mother and drew back the chain,
And opened the door to the wind and the rain.

III *Repentance*

"I am not guiltless, my hands not blameless,
But my heart repents in no wise."
And he knelt down at the threshold,
Lay down and would not rise.

"Seven times have I proved my falseness,
Seven times blasphemed the Name,
And the heavens above bear witness
That I was always to blame.

"The heavens above bear witness
That sin is bone of my bone,
And that I shall still prove faithless,
For I am the prodigal son."

The sister stood in the doorway
And weeping bowed her head;
The bride in the open doorway
Wrung hands as if for the dead.

The brother stayed in his chamber,
For what had he to say,
And spied from his dark chamber
On his brother where he lay.

But the mother raised her face,
And her face like sunlight shone,
"What matters whether evil or good,
Since you have returned, my son.

"Your father will never forgive you
Who chose the forbidden path.
But rise and receive the blessing
Of your father's loving wrath."

Translated from the Hebrew
by Robert Friend

LÉOPOLD SÉDAR SENGHOR

Return of the Prodigal Son

(guimm* *for a* kora†)

> to Jacques Maguilen Senghor, my nephew

I

And my heart once again on the threshold of stone under the
    portal of honor.
And a tremor stirs the warm ashes of the lightning-eyed Man,
    my father.
On my hunger, the dust of sixteen years of wandering
And the uncertainty of Europe's many roads
And the noise of sprawling cities, and towns lashed by the waves
Of a thousand passions in my head.
My heart is still pure as the East Wind in March.

II

I challenge my blood in this head empty of ideas, in this belly
Abandoned by courageous muscles.
Guide me by the golden note of the silent flute, guide me,
Herdsman, brother who shared my childhood dreams, naked
    under his milk belt
And with the flame tree's flower on his brow.
And pierce, herdsman, just pierce with a long surreal note
This tottering house where termites have eaten away windows
    and inhabitants.
And my heart once again under the great dwelling built by
    the Man's pride.
And my heart once again on the tomb where he has piously
    laid his ancient lineage to rest.
He needs no paper, only the troubador's musical page
And the red-gold stylus of his tongue.

---

*A song or poem.
†An instrument with many strings stretched along a wooden arm and extending from a
hollowed calabash.

III

How vast, how void is the courtyard smelling of nothingness,
Like the plain in the dry season trembling with emptiness,
But what woodcutting storm felled the secular tree?
An entire people had subsisted on its shade on the round terrace,
A whole household with stableboys and artisans and family
	herdsmen
On the red terrace that protected the surging sea of herds
On the great days of fire and blood.
Or is it now a district struck by four-engined eagles
And by lions of bombs with such powerful leaps?

IV

And my heart once again on the steps of the high house.
I lay on the ground at your feet in the dust of my respect,
At your feet, Ancestors who are present, who proudly dominate
The great room of your masks defying Time.
Faithful servant of my childhood, here are my feet
Caked with the mud of Civilization.
Only pure water on my feet, servant, and only their white soles
	on the still mats.
Peace, peace, peace, my Fathers, on the Prodigal Son's head.

V

You among them all, Elephant of Mbissel, shower your troubador
	poet with friendship
And he partakes with you of the dishes of honor, the oil
	highlighting the lips,
And the river horses, gifts from the Sine‡ kings, masters of millet,
Masters of palms, the Sine kings who had planted in Diakhaw

---

‡Senghor's native region in Senegal.

The legitimate force of their lance. And among them all,
This Mbogou, of desert-colored skin; and the *Guelwârs*§
Shed libations of tears at his departure
Pure rain of dew as when the Sun's death bleeds on the ocean
　　plain
And on the waves of dead warriors.

VI

Elephant of Mbissel, through your ears invisible to our eyes,
Let my Ancestors hear my reverent prayer.
May you be blessed, my Fathers, may you be blessed!
Merchants and bankers, lords of gold and the outskirts of town
Where a chimney forest grows
—They have bought their nobility and blackened their mother's
　　womb
The merchants and bankers have banished me from the Nation.
And they have carved "Mercenary" on my honorable weapons
And they knew I asked for no pay, only ten cents
To cradle the smoke of my dreams and milk to wash away my
　　blue bitterness.
If I have planted my loyalty back in the fields of defeat,
It is because God has struck France with his leaden hand.
May you be blessed, my Fathers, may you be blessed.
You who have endured scorn and mockery, polite offenses,
Discreet slurs and taboos and segregation.
And you have torn from this too-loving heart
The ties that bind it to the world's pulse.
May you be blessed, you who refused to let hatred turn a man's
　　heart
To stone. You know that I have made friends with the forbidden
　　princes

§ Noble descendents of the Manding conquerors.

Of intellect and the princes of form, that I have eaten the bread
That brings hunger to countless armies of workers
And those without work, that I dreamt of a world of sun
In fraternity with my blue-eyed brothers.

VII

Elephant of Mbissel, I applaud the emptiness of shops around the
     noble house.
I applaud joyfully! Long live the merchant's bankruptcy!
I applaud this strip of sea abandoned by white wings—
The crocodiles now hunt deep in the woods
And the sea cows graze in peace!
I burn down the *seco!* The pyramid of peanuts towering above the
     land
And the hard wharf, an implacable will upon the sea.
But I bring back to life the sound of the herds, their neighing and
     bellowing,
The sound modulating the flutes and conch shells in the evening
     moonlight
I bring back the procession of servant girls on the dew
And the great calabashes of milk, steady, on their rhythmic,
     swaying hips.
I bring back to life the caravan of donkeys and camels
Smelling of millet and rice
In the glittering mirrors, in the tolling of faces and silver bells.
I bring back to life all my earthly virtues!

VIII

Elephant of Mbissel, hear my reverent prayer.
Give me the skilled knowledge of the great Timbuktu doctors,
Give me Soni Ali's strong will, born of the Lion's slobber—
A tidal wave to the conquest of a continent.

"A gigantic mound of peanuts awaiting sale.

Blow upon me the Keïtas' wisdom.

Give me the *Guelwâr*'s courage, gird my loins with the strength of
    a *tyedo*.#

Give me the chance to die for the struggles of my people,

And if necessary in the odor of gunpowder and cannon.

Preserve and root in my freed heart the foremost love of my
    people.

Make me your Master Linguist; No, no,

Appoint me his ambassador.

IX

May you be blessed, my Fathers, who bless the Prodigal Son!

I want to see again the room on the right where the women
    worked,

Where I played with the doves and my brothers, sons of the Lion.

Ah! to sleep once again in the cool bed of my childhood

Ah! to have loving black hands once again tuck me in at night,

And see once again my mother's white smile.

Tomorrow I will continue on my way to Europe, to the embassy,

Already homesick for my black Land.

Translated from the French
by Melvin Dixon

#A member of the slave caste.

MARINA TSVETAYEVA

And, Not Crying in Vain

And, not crying in vain
About father and mother—you must arise, God save you,
On the highways,
In the night—without a dog or lantern.

Night has a thievish maw.
It will swallow your shame and cut you off from God.
Yet it will teach you
To sing and, smiling into someone's eyes, to steal.

And to call someone
With a long whistle, at black crossroads,
And to kiss others' submissive
Wives under the trees.

Whether the field fills up with ice
Or grain—still on the roads, it's wonderful!—
Only in the story does the prodigal
Son return to his father's house.

10 October 1916

Translated from the Russian
by Nancy Pollak

IVAN BUNIN

Flowers, and tall-stalked grasses, and a bee

Flowers, and tall-stalked grasses, and a bee,
and azure, blaze of the meridian . . .
The time will come, the Lord will ask his prodigal son:
"In your life on earth, were you happy?"

And I'll forget it all, only remembering those
meadow paths among tall spears of grass,
and clasped against the knees of mercy I
will not respond, choked off by tears of joy.

14.VIII.18

Translated from the Russian
by David Curzon and Vladislav I. Guerassev

THE PARABLE OF THE UNJUST STEWARD

LUKE 16:1–9

16 He also said to the disciples, "There was a rich man who had a steward, and charges were brought to him that this man was wasting his goods. ²And he called him and said to him, 'What is this that I hear about you? Turn in the account of your stewardship, for you can no longer be steward.' ³And the steward said to himself, 'What shall I do, since my master is taking the stewardship away from me? I am not strong enough to dig, and I am ashamed to beg. ⁴I have decided what to do, so that people may receive me into their houses when I am put out of the stewardship.' ⁵So, summoning his master's debtors one by one, he said to the first, 'How much do you owe my master?' ⁶He said, 'A hundred measures of oil.' And he said to him, 'Take your bill, and sit down quickly and write fifty.' ⁷Then he said to another, 'And how much do you owe?' He said, 'A hundred measures of wheat.' He said to him, 'Take your bill, and write eighty.' ⁸The master commended the dishonest steward for his shrewdness; for the sons of this world[w] are more shrewd in dealing with their own generation than the sons of light. ⁹And I tell you, make friends for yourselves by means of unrighteous mammon,[a] so that when it fails they may receive you into the eternal habitations.["]

---

[w] Greek *age*
[a] *Mammon* is a Semitic word for money or riches

ERNESTO CARDENAL

Unrighteous Mammon (Luke 16:9)

In respect of riches, then, just or unjust,
of goods be they ill-gotten or well-gotten:
                    All riches are unjust.
All goods,
                    ill-gotten.
If not by you, by others.
Your title deeds may be in order. But
did you buy your land from its true owner?
And he from its true owner? And the latter . . . ?
Though your title go back to the grant of a king
                    was
the land ever the king's?
Has no one ever been deprived of it?
And the money you receive legitimately now
from client or Bank or National Funds
                    or from the U.S. Treasury,
was it ill-gotten at no point? Yet
do not think that in the Perfect Communist State
Christ's parables will have lost relevance
Or Luke 16:9 have lost validity
                    and riches be no longer UNJUST
or that you will no longer have a duty to distribute riches!

Translated from the Spanish
by Robert Pring-Mill

THE PARABLE OF THE RICH MAN
AND LAZARUS

LUKE 16:19–26

19 "There was a rich man, who was clothed in purple and fine linen and who feasted sumptuously every day. ²⁰And at his gate lay a poor man named Laz′arus, full of sores, ²¹who desired to be fed with what fell from the rich man's table; moreover the dogs came and licked his sores. ²²The poor man died and was carried by the angels to Abraham's bosom. The rich man also died and was buried; ²³and in Hades, being in torment, he lifted up his eyes, and saw Abraham far off and Laz′arus in his bosom. ²⁴And he called out, 'Father Abraham, have mercy upon me, and send Laz′arus to dip the end of his finger in water and cool my tongue; for I am in anguish in this flame.' ²⁵But Abraham said, 'Son, remember that you in your lifetime received your good things, and Laz′arus in like manner evil things; but now he is comforted here, and you are in anguish. ²⁶And besides all this, between us and you a great chasm has been fixed, in order that those who would pass from here to you may not be able, and none may cross from there to us.' ["]

19: The *rich man*, though unnamed, is commonly called "Dives" (Latin for "rich man").

ROBERT FROST

In Divés' Dive

It is late at night and still I am losing,
But still I am steady and unaccusing.

As long as the Declaration guards
My right to be equal in number of cards,

It is nothing to me who runs the Dive.
Let's have a look at another five.

THE RAISING OF LAZARUS

JOHN 11:30–44

30 Now Jesus had not yet come to the village, but was still in the place where Martha had met him. ³¹When the Jews who were with her in the house, consoling her, saw Mary rise quickly and go out, they followed her, supposing that she was going to the tomb to weep there. ³²Then Mary, when she came where Jesus was and saw him, fell at his feet, saying to him, "Lord, if you had been here, my brother would not have died." ³³When Jesus saw her weeping, and the Jews who came with her also weeping, he was deeply moved in spirit and troubled; ³⁴and he said, "Where have you laid him?" They said to him, "Lord, come and see." ³⁵Jesus wept. ³⁶So the Jews said, "See how he loved him!" ³⁷But some of them said, "Could not he who opened the eyes of the blind man have kept this man from dying?"

38 Then Jesus, deeply moved again, came to the tomb; it was a cave, and a stone lay upon it. ³⁹Jesus said, "Take away the stone." Martha, the sister of the dead man, said to him, "Lord, by this time there will be an odor, for he has been dead four days." ⁴⁰Jesus said to her, "Did I not tell you that if you would believe you would see the glory of God?" ⁴¹So they took away the stone. And Jesus lifted up his eyes and said, "Father, I thank thee that thou hast heard me. ⁴²I knew that thou hearest me always, but I have said this on account of the people standing by, that they may believe that thou didst send me." ⁴³When he had said this, he cried with a loud voice, "Laz'arus, come out." ⁴⁴The dead man came out, his hands and feet bound with bandages, and his face wrapped with a cloth. Jesus said to them, "Unbind him, and let him go."

RAINER MARIA RILKE

The Raising of Lazarus

As for the riffraff, the needed act, the one
they clearly wanted, was some sign that shrieked.
For Martha and Mary, though, he'd dreamed
it would have been enough for them to see
he *could*. But none had trust in him,
all said: Why come *now*, Lord?
So he went there to execute
the illicit act on Nature's peacefulness.
In fury. Eyes squeezed tight, he asked
about the grave. He suffered it.
To them it looked as if he was in tears;
they pushed and shoved in curiosity.
While walking it still seemed to him some immense
atrocious game of an experiment,
and abruptly there erupted within him
the fierce flame of an opposition to
all aspects of their difference, to
the way in which they lived and died,
and with enmity in every limb of his
he yelled, hoarsely: Lift the stone!
A voice then shouted he'll be stinking now
(since he'd been down four days)—but he
stood straight, filled with that gesture
which rose in him so heavily, and heavily
he raised his hand—(no hand ever
was raised more slowly than that hand)
until it stayed and shone in air;
and there, above, it clutched as if a claw:
for he had horror now, that all the dead
would want to come again through that

shaft of a vault in which a larval thing
was gathered upward from its supine state—
but then it merely stood in a slant of light
and one could see: this vague and inexact
life had once again accepted it.

Translated from the German
by David Curzon and Will Alexander Washburn

WILLIAM BUTLER YEATS

from *"Calvary"*

. . .

[A player with the mask of Lazarus has entered.]
Lazarus.   He raised me up.
   I am the man that died and was raised up;
   I am called Lazarus.
Christ.   Seeing that you died,
   Lay in the tomb four days and were raised up,
   You will not mock at me.
Lazarus.   For four whole days
   I had been dead and I was lying still
   In an old comfortable mountain cavern
         When you came climbing there with a great crowd
   And dragged me to the light.
Christ.   I called your name:
   'Lazarus, come out', I said, and you came out
   Bound up in cloths, your face bound in a cloth.
Lazarus. You took my death, give me your death instead.
Christ. I gave you life.

Lazarus.　　　But death is what I ask.
　　Alive I never could escape your love,
　　And when I sickened towards my death I thought,
　　'I'll to the desert, or chuckle in a corner,
　　Mere ghost, a solitary thing.' I died
　　And saw no more until I saw you stand
　　In the opening of the tomb; 'Come out!' you called;
　　You dragged me to the light as boys drag out
　　A rabbit when they have dug its hole away;
　　And now with all the shouting at your heels
　　You travel towards the death I am denied.
　　And that is why I have hurried to this road
　　And claimed your death.
Christ.　　　　　But I have conquered death,
　　And all the dead shall be raised up again.
Lazarus. Then what I heard is true. I thought to die
　　When my allotted years ran out again;
　　And that, being gone, you could not hinder it;
　　But now you will blind with light the solitude
　　That death has made; you will disturb that corner
　　Where I had thought I might lie safe for ever.
Christ. I do my Father's will.
Lazarus.　　　　And not your own;
　　And I was free four days, four days being dead.
　　Climb up to Calvary, but turn your eyes
　　From Lazarus that cannot find a tomb
　　Although he search all height and depth: make way,
　　Make way for Lazarus that must go search
　　Among the desert places where there is nothing
　　But howling wind and solitary birds.　　[*He goes out.*]
. . .

NICANOR PARRA

The Anti-Lazarus

Lazarus
don't come forth from the grave
resurrection won't do a thing for you
a moment's glory
                  and then
                              the same old routine
don't do it old friend don't do it

pride and blood and greed
the tyranny of sexual desire
the way women make you suffer

the enigma of time
the contradictions of space

think it over Lazarus think it over

don't you remember the way it was?
how you blew up at every little thing
and cursed everybody in sight?
everything got under your skin
you couldn't stand it anymore
you even despised your own shadow

your memory's going old friend your memory's going

your heart was a rubbish heap
—that's what you wrote—I'm quoting now—
there was nothing left of your soul

then why come back to Dante's inferno?
why play the comedy again?
some divine comedy—some joke!
it's only fireworks—illusions—
bait for catching greedy little mice—
a fatal blunder!

you don't know how well off you are
you have everything you need in your grave
relax take it easy down there

hello—hello—are you listening to me?

who wouldn't prefer
the earth's embrace
to a gloomy whore's caresses

nobody in his right mind
unless he's in league with the devil

keep on sleeping old friend keep on sleeping
free of the petty doubts that haunted you
lord and master of your own coffin
in the stillness of perfect night
free as a bird
as if you'd never walked among the living

whatever you do don't rise up from the grave
why should you be nervous

like the poet once said
you have your whole death in front of you

Translated from the Spanish
by Edith Grossman

ÁGNES NEMES NAGY

Lazarus

He sat up slowly, and around his left side
all his long life's muscles ached.
His death was torn from him like caked
gauze. Rising was as hard as having died.

Translated from the Hungarian
by Frederic Will

THE EYE OF A NEEDLE

MATTHEW 19:16–24
(Parallel texts: Mark 10:17–25; Luke 18:18–25)

16 And behold, one came up to him, saying, "Teacher, what good deed must I do, to have eternal life?" [17]And he said to him, "Why do you ask me about what is good? One there is who is good. If you would enter life, keep the commandments." [18]He said to him, "Which?" And Jesus said, "You shall not kill, You shall not commit adultery, You shall not steal, You shall not bear false witness, [19]Honor your father and mother, and, You shall love your neighbor as yourself." [20]The young man said to him, "All these I have observed; what do I still lack?" [21]Jesus said to him, "If you would be perfect, go, sell what you possess and give to the poor, and you will have treasure in heaven; and come, follow me." [22]When the young man heard this he went away sorrowful; for he had great possessions.

23 And Jesus said to his disciples, "Truly, I say to you, it will be hard for a rich man to enter the kingdom of heaven. [24]Again I tell you, it is easier for a camel to go through the eye of a needle than for a rich man to enter the kingdom of God."

16: Lev.18.5. The question concerns the way of life which Jesus will guarantee as satisfying God.
18: Ex.20.12–16; Dt.5.16–20.
19: Lev.19.18.

ANNA KAMIENSKA

Things of This World

Theresa of Avila surely had a gold thimble
and John of the Cross suffering from sleepless fears
lit the wick in a clay lamp
and by its light the stool grew on his cell's wall

From earth's clay none can free themselves
and the spirit has some kinship with clay
therefore absolve me God from objects
which lead me humbly
to the rim of the abyss only to leave me there
But I don't hold it against my father's violin
my mother's glasses   my grandmother's cane
they walked with them as much as they could
demanding nothing   without moaning or complaint

Taking leave from the scored edge of a table
usually isn't easy   from a low stool for your feet
from an old porcelain inkpot
I speak to them with the tongue of love
so they won't get covered up with an icy glaze
I feed them with radiance   with a lamp's light
they like it knowing they will endure
calm and poor like the camel in the Gospel
who pushes his hump to heaven through the needle's eye

Translated from the Polish
by David Curzon and Grażyna Drabik

ENTERING JERUSALEM

MATTHEW 21:1–11
(Parallel texts: Mark 11:1–10; Luke 19:28–38; John 12:12–19)

21 And when they drew near to Jerusalem and came to Beth'phage, to the Mount of Olives, then Jesus sent two disciples, ²saying to them, "Go into the village opposite you, and immediately you will find an ass tied, and a colt with her; untie them and bring them to me. ³If any one says anything to you, you shall say, 'The Lord has need of them,' and he will send them immediately." ⁴This took place to fulfill what was spoken by the prophet, saying,

⁵"Tell the daughter of Zion,

Behold, your king is coming to you,

humble, and mounted on an ass,

and on a colt, the foal of an ass."

⁶The disciples went and did as Jesus had directed them; ⁷they brought the ass and the colt, and put their garments on them, and he sat thereon. ⁸Most of the crowd spread their garments on the road, and others cut branches from the trees and spread them on the road. ⁹And the crowds that went before him and that followed him shouted, "Hosanna to the Son of David! Blessed is he who comes in the name of the Lord! Hosanna in the highest!" ¹⁰And when he entered Jerusalem, all the city was stirred, saying, "Who is this?" ¹¹And the crowds said, "This is the prophet Jesus from Nazareth of Galilee."

5: Is.62.11; Zech.9.9. The Hebrew text refers not to two animals but to one. The reference to the two in v. 7 may have arisen through misunderstanding the form of Hebrew poetic expression in Zech.9.9.

8: Tokens of honor (2 Kg.9.13).

9: Ps.118.26. *Hosanna,* originally a Hebrew invocation addressed to God, meaning, "O save!"; later it was used as a cry of joyous acclamation.

BORIS PASTERNAK

The Evil Days

When, in that final week,
He was entering Jerusalem
They thundered Hosannas,
And greeted Him with branches.

Now the days are ominous and grim,
Hearts are no longer stirred by love,
Eyebrows are knit in contempt.
And now the epilogue, the end.

With all their leaden weight
The heavens lay on the courtyards.
Pharisees looked for proof against Him,
Yet wheedled Him like foxes.

And the dark forces of the Temple
Gave Him to rogues for judgement,
And as fervently as they had praised
They cursed Him now.

The rabble from the neighborhood
Was peering through the gates,
They jostled, in wait for the outcome,
And bustled about, back and forth.

And a whisper crept round there,
As did rumors from every side.
He recalled the flight to Egypt
And His childhood, but now as in a dream.

He recollected the majestic slope
In the desert, and the heights
From which Satan had tempted Him
With all the kingdoms of the world.

And the wedding feast at Cana,
The guests amazed by miracle.
And the sea on which, in a fog,
He'd walked to the boat as on dry land.

And the gathering of poor in a hovel,
And His going down to a cellar with a candle
Which suddenly, in fright, went out
As the resurrected man was standing up . . .

Translated from the Russian
by Nina Kossman

G. K. CHESTERTON

The Donkey

When fishes flew and forests walked
    And figs grew upon thorn,
Some moment when the moon was blood
    Then surely I was born.

With monstrous head and sickening cry
    And ears like errant wings,
The devil's walking parody
    On all four-footed things.

The tattered outlaw of the earth,
    Of ancient crooked will;
Starve, scourge, deride me: I am dumb,
    I keep my secret still.

Fools! For I also had my hour;
    One far fierce hour and sweet:
There was a shout about my ears,
    And palms before my feet.

THE LAST DAY OF PUBLIC TEACHING

MATTHEW 21:18–22
(Parallel text: Mark 11:12–26)

18 In the morning, as he was returning to the city, he was hungry. ¹⁹And seeing a fig tree by the wayside he went to it, and found nothing on it but leaves only. And he said to it, "May no fruit ever come from you again!" And the fig tree withered at once. ²⁰When the disciples saw it they marveled, saying, "How did the fig tree wither at once?" ²¹And Jesus answered them, "Truly, I say to you, if you have faith and never doubt, you will not only do what has been done to the fig tree, but even if you say to this mountain, 'Be taken up and cast into the sea,' it will be done. ²²And whatever you ask in prayer, you will receive, if you have faith."

DONALD HALL

A Small Fig Tree

I am dead, to be sure,
for thwarting Christ's pleasure,
Jesus Christ called Saviour.

I was a small fig tree.
Unjust it seems to me
that I should withered be.

If justice sits with God,
Christ is cruel Herod
and I by magic dead.

If there is no justice
where great Jehovah is,
I will the devil kiss.

BORIS PASTERNAK

The Miracle*

He was walking from Bethany to Jerusalem,
Brooding over sad premonitions.

The sun scorched the slope's prickly shrubs,
No smoke was rising over a nearby hut,
The air was hot and the reeds motionless,
And the calm of the Dead Sea lay still.

And with a bitterness rivalling the sea's,
He walked with a small throng of clouds
Along a dusty road, to somebody's backyard,
On His way to a gathering of disciples.

And so immersed was He in His thoughts,
That the field, dejected, sent off a wormwood smell.
All was still. He stood alone in the midst of it,
While the land lay prostrate in swoon.
All became muddled; the heat, the desert,
The lizards, the springs, the streams.

A fig tree rose not too far off,
Fruitless, nothing but branches and leaves.
And He said to it: "Of what use are you?
What joy does your stupor bring me?

"I thirst and hunger, yet you stand barren,
My meeting you is joyless as granite.
O, how offensive and ungifted you are!
Remain as you are, then, till the end of time."

*A note on this poem can be found on page 269.

A tremor of condemnation ran through the tree,
Like a spark of lightning down a rod.
The fig tree was reduced to ashes.

If only a moment of freedom had been given
To the leaves, the branches, roots, trunk,
The laws of nature could have intervened.
But a miracle is a miracle, and a miracle is God.
When we're in confusion, in the midst of disorder,
It overtakes us instantly, by surprise.

Translated from the Russian
by Nina Kossman

MATTHEW 22:1–14
(Parallel text: Luke 14:16–24)

22 And again Jesus spoke to them in parables, saying, 2"The kingdom of heaven may be compared to a king who gave a marriage feast for his son, 3and sent his servants to call those who were invited to the marriage feast; but they would not come. 4Again he sent other servants, saying, 'Tell those who are invited, Behold, I have made ready my dinner, my oxen and my fat calves are killed, and everything is ready; come to the marriage feast.' 5But they made light of it and went off, one to his farm, another to his business, 6while the rest seized his servants, treated them shamefully, and killed them. 7The king was angry, and he sent his troops and destroyed those murderers and burned their city. 8Then he said to his servants, 'The wedding is ready, but those invited were not worthy. 9Go therefore to the thoroughfares, and invite to the marriage feast as many as you find.' 10And those servants went out into the streets and gathered all whom they found, both bad and good; so the wedding hall was filled with guests.

11 "But when the king came in to look at the guests, he saw there a man who had no wedding garment; 12and he said to him, 'Friend, how did you get in here without a wedding garment?' And he was speechless. 13Then the king said to the attendants, 'Bind him hand and foot, and cast him into the outer darkness; there men will weep and gnash their teeth.' 14For many are called, but few are chosen.''

EDWIN ARLINGTON ROBINSON

*Many Are Called**

The Lord Apollo, who has never died,
Still holds alone his immemorial reign,
Supreme in an impregnable domain
That with his magic he has fortified;
And though melodious multitudes have tried
In ecstasy, in anguish, and in vain,
With invocation sacred and profane
To lure him, even the loudest are outside.

Only at unconjectured intervals,
By will of him on whom no man may gaze,
By word of him whose law no man has read,
A questing light may rift the sullen walls,
To cling where mostly its infrequent rays
Fall golden on the patience of the dead.

*A note on this poem can be found on page 269.

MATTHEW 22:15–22
(Parallel texts: Mark 12:13–17; Luke 20:20–26)

15 Then the Pharisees went and took counsel how to entangle him in his talk. ¹⁶And they sent their disciples to him, along with the Hero'dians, saying, "Teacher, we know that you are true, and teach the way of God truthfully, and care for no man; for you do not regard the position of men. ¹⁷Tell us, then, what you think. Is it lawful to pay taxes to Caesar, or not?" ¹⁸But Jesus, aware of their malice, said, "Why put me to the test, you hypocrites? ¹⁹Show me the money for the tax." And they brought him a coin. ²⁰And Jesus said to them, "Whose likeness and inscription is this?" ²¹They said, "Caesar's." Then he said to them, "Render therefore to Caesar the things that are Caesar's, and to God the things that are God's." ²²When they heard it, they marveled; and they left him and went away.

DESANKA MAKSIMOVIĆ

For the Barren Woman

I am asking for understanding
for the women who have not given
unto God the things that are God's
nor unto Caesar the things that are Caesar's
who have never put asleep
a child in the cradle
for those who have not been blessed,
for the women
who carry the placards
with dreams and reveries
in whose blood-stream only songs murmur,
for those whose hearts are made fruitful
by the fragrance and murmur of water,
whose embraces are full of clouds only,
who, like birds, make their nests high in the air,
and give birth to water flowers of beauty.
For everyone who breaks the ranks
of the routine,
unaccustomed,
who like enchanted strays
somewhere away from the old road,
I am asking clemency and pardon, dear emperor,
for all those who have since their early youth
opted for the kingdom of poetry,
who flutter all the time like birch trees,
and are ravished by moonshine like a boat,
for Jeremiahs,
for St. Teresas
for every Sappho
and every Joan of Arc,
for all the enraptured and unfinished,
and for me.

Translated from the Serbo-Croatian by Ivo Soljan

JOHN 12:24–25

²⁴ Truly, truly, I say to you, unless a grain of wheat falls into the earth and dies, it remains alone; but if it dies, it bears much fruit. ²⁵He who loves his life loses it, and he who hates his life in this world will keep it for eternal life.

PIER PAOLO PASOLINI

The Day of My Death

> Except a corn of wheat fall into the ground and die, it abideth alone: but if
> it die, it bringeth forth much fruit. —JOHN 12:24 (cited by Dostoyevsky)

In a city, Trieste or Udine,
   down in a valley of lime trees,
when the leaves
   change color . . .
   a person lived,
with the strength of a young man
        in the heart of the world,
and he gave, to those few men
he knew, everything.

Then, for love of those
   who were boys
like him—until shortly before
   the stars changed
   their light on his head—
he would have wanted to give his life
        for the whole unknown world,
he, unknown, little saint,
seed fallen in the field.

And instead he wrote
   poems of holiness
believing that in this way
   his heart would become larger.

   The days have passed
in a labor which ruined
        the holiness of his heart:
the seed hasn't died
and he has remained alone.

Translated from the Italian by Max Hayward and Lawrence R. Smith

MATTHEW 24:15–31
(Parallel texts: Mark 13:14–27; Luke 21:20–28)

15 "So when you see the desolating sacrilege spoken of by the prophet Daniel, standing in the holy place (let the reader understand), [16]then let those who are in Judea flee to the mountains; [17]let him who is on the housetop not go down to take what is in his house; [18]and let him who is in the field not turn back to take his mantle. [19]And alas for those who are with child and for those who give suck in those days! [20]Pray that your flight may not be in winter or on a sabbath. [21]For then there will be great tribulation, such as has not been from the beginning of the world until now, no, and never will be. [22]And if those days had not been shortened, no human being would be saved; but for the sake of the elect those days will be shortened. [23]Then if any one says to you, 'Lo, here is the Christ!' or 'There he is!' do not believe it. [24]For false Christs and false prophets will arise and show great signs and wonders, so as to lead astray, if possible, even the elect. [25]Lo, I have told you beforehand. [26]So, if they say to you, 'Lo, he is in the wilderness,' do not go out; if they say, 'Lo, he is in the inner rooms,' do not believe it. [27]For as the lightning comes from the east and shines as far as the west, so will be the coming of the Son of man. [28]Wherever the body is, there the eagles[z] will be gathered together.

29 "Immediately after the tribulations of those days the sun will be darkened, and the moon will not give its light, and the stars will fall from heaven, and the powers of the heavens will be shaken; [30]then will appear the sign of the Son of man in heaven,

[z] Or *vultures*
15: Dan.9.27; 11.31; 12.11. 21: Dan.12.1; J1.2.2. 28: Job 39.30. 29–31: The language here is drawn from the Old Testament; God's victory over sin is to be established by the Son of man whom he sends (Is.13:10; 34.4; Ezek.32.7; J2.1.10–11; Zeph.1.15). 30: Dan.7.13. 31: Is.27.13; Zech.2.10; 9.14.

and then all the tribes of the earth will mourn, and they will see the Son of man coming on the clouds of heaven with power and great glory; [31]and he will send out his angels with a loud trumpet call, and they will gather his elect from the four winds, from one end of heaven to the other.["]

WILLIAM BUTLER YEATS

The Second Coming*

Turning and turning in the widening gyre
The falcon cannot hear the falconer;
Things fall apart; the centre cannot hold;
Mere anarchy is loosed upon the world,
The blood-dimmed tide is loosed, and everywhere
The ceremony of innocence is drowned;
The best lack all conviction, while the worst
Are full of passionate intensity.

Surely some revelation is at hand;
Surely the Second Coming is at hand.
The Second Coming! Hardly are those words out
When a vast image out of *Spiritus Mundi*
Troubles my sight: somewhere in sands of the desert
A shape with lion body and the head of a man,
A gaze blank and pitiless as the sun,
Is moving its slow thighs, while all about it
Reel shadows of the indignant desert birds.
The darkness drops again; but now I know
That twenty centuries of stony sleep
Were vexed to nightmare by a rocking cradle,
And what rough beast, its hour come round at last,
Slouches towards Bethlehem to be born?

*A note on this poem can be found on page 269.

MATTHEW 25:14–30
(Parallel text: Luke 19:12–27)

14 "For it will be as when a man going on a journey called
his servants and entrusted to them his property; ¹⁵to one he gave
five talents, to another two, to another one, to each according to
his ability. Then he went away. ¹⁶He who had received the five
talents went at once and traded with them; and he made five tal-
ents more. ¹⁷So also, he who had the two talents made two talents
more. ¹⁸But he who had received the one talent went and dug in
the ground and hid his master's money. ¹⁹Now after a long time
the master of those servants came and settled accounts with them.
²⁰And he who had received the five talents came foward, bringing
five talents more, saying, 'Master, you delivered to me five talents;
here I have made five talents more.' ²¹His master said to him, 'Well
done, good and faithful servant; you have been faithful over a
little, I will set you over much; enter into the joy of your master.'
. . .

²⁴ He also who had received the one talent came foward, saying,
'Master, I knew you to be a hard man, reaping where you did not
sow, and gathering where you did not winnow; ²⁵so I was afraid,
and I went and hid your talent in the ground. Here you have what
is yours.' ²⁶But his master answered him, 'You wicked and slothful
servant! You knew that I reap where I have not sowed, and gather
where I have not winnowed? ²⁷Then you ought to have invested
my money with the bankers, and at my coming I should have re-
ceived what was my own with interest. ²⁸So take the talent from
him, and give it to him who has the ten talents. ²⁹For to everyone
who has will more be given, and he will have abundance; but from
him who has not, even what he has will be taken away. ³⁰And cast
the worthless servant into the outer darkness; there men will weep
and gnash their teeth.' "

JORGE LUIS BORGES

Matthew XXV:30*

The main bridge of Constitution, and at my feet
The din of trains that knit up labyrinths of iron.
Smoke and hisses climb into the night
Which suddenly becomes the Last Judgment. From
    the invisible horizon,
From the center of my being, an infinite voice
Spoke these things (these things, and not these words,
which are my poor temporal translation of a single word):
—Stars, bread, libraries of the orient and occident,
Cards, chessboards, galleries, skylights and cellars,
A human body with which to walk the earth,
Fingernails that grow in the night, and in death,
Shadow that forgets, mirrors busy redoubling,
Cadences of music, most gentle of the forms of time,
Borders of Brazil and Uruguay, horses and mornings,
A bronze weight and a copy of the Grettir Saga,
Algebra and fire, the charge at Junín in your blood,
Days more crowded than Balzac, the scent of honeysuckle,
Love and the eve of love and unendurable recollections,
The dream like a buried treasure, generous luck,
And memory, that man sees only with vertigo,
All this was given to you, and, as well,
The ancient nourishment of heroes:
Betrayal, defeat, humiliation.
In vain have we squandered the ocean on you,
In vain the sun, seen by Whitman's wonderful eyes;
You have spent the years and they've spent you,
And yet you have not written the poem.

1953

Translated from the Spanish
by David Curzon

*A note on this poem can be found on page 269.

THE LAST SUPPER

MATTHEW 26:17–29
(Parallel texts: Mark 14:12–25; Luke 22:7–20; John 13:1–20)

17 Now on the first day of Unleavened Bread the disciples came to Jesus, saying, "Where will you have us prepare for you to eat the passover?" [18]He said, "Go into the city to a certain one, and say to him, 'The Teacher says, My time is at hand; I will keep the passover at your house with my disciples.' " [19]And the disciples did as Jesus had directed them, and they prepared the passover.

20 When it was evening, he sat at table with the twelve disciples;[e] [21]and as they were eating, he said, "Truly, I say to you, one of you will betray me." [22]And they were very sorrowful, and began to say to him one after another, "Is it I, Lord?" [23]He answered, "He who has dipped his hand in the dish with me, will betray me. [24]The Son of man goes as it is written of him, but woe to that man by whom the Son of man is betrayed! It would have been better for that man if he had not been born." [25]Judas, who betrayed him, said, "Is it I, Master?"[f] He said to him, "You have said so."

26 Now as they were eating, Jesus took bread, and blessed, and broke it, and gave it to the disciples and said, "Take, eat; this is my body." [27]And he took a cup, and when he had given thanks he gave it to them, saying, "Drink of it, all of you; [28]for this is my blood of the[g] covenant, which is poured out for many for the forgiveness of sins. [29]I tell you I shall not drink again of this fruit of the vine until that day when I drink it new with you in my Father's kingdom."

[e] Other authorities omit *disciples*
[f] Or *Rabbi*
[g] Other ancient authorities insert *new*

19: Dt.16.5–8.   24: Ps.41.9.   28: Ex.24.6–8.

RAINER MARIA RILKE

The Last Supper

They are assembled, astounded, bewildered,
round him who, like a sage centered at last,
withdraws from those to whom he once belonged
and flows beyond them as some foreigner.
The former solitude comes over him
which raised him to perform his profound acts;
again he'll wander in the olive grove,
and those who love him will now run from him.

He summons them to the final meal
and (as a shot shoos birds from sheaves)
he shoos their hand from bread
with his word: they flutter up to him;
they flap about the table anxiously
searching for some way out. But *he,*
like an evening hour, is everywhere.

Translated from the German
by David Curzon and Will Alexander Washburn

DYLAN THOMAS

This Bread I Break

This bread I break was once the oat,
This wine upon a foreign tree
Plunged in its fruit;
Man in the day or wind at night
Laid the crops low, broke the grape's joy.

Once in this wine the summer blood
Knocked in the flesh that decked the vine,
Once in this bread
The oat was merry in the wind;
Man broke the sun, pulled the wind down.

This flesh you break, this blood you let
Make desolation in the vein,
Were oat and grape
Born of the sensual root and sap;
My wine you drink, my bread you snap.

JACQUES PRÉVERT

Last Supper

They are at table
They do not touch their plates
They don't feel all that well
And their plates stand up straight
Vertically behind their heads.

Translated from the French
by Jeffrey Fiskin

21 When Jesus had thus said, he was troubled in spirit, and testified, and said, Verily, verily, I say unto you, that one of you shall betray me.

22 Then the disciples looked one on another, doubting of whom he spake.

23 Now there was leaning on Jesus' bosom one of his disciples, whom Jesus loved.

24 Simon Peter therefore beckoned to him, that he should ask who it should be of whom he spake.

25 He then lying on Jesus' breast saith unto him, Lord, who is it?

26 Jesus answered, He it is, to whom I shall give a sop, when I have dipped it. And when he had dipped the sop, he gave it to Judas Iscariot, the son of Simon.

27 And after the sop Satan entered into him. Then said Jesus unto him, That thou doest, do quickly.

28 Now no man at the table knew for what intent he spake this unto him.

29 For some of them thought, because Judas had the bag, that Jesus had said unto him, Buy those things that we have need of against the feast; or, that he should give something to the poor.

30 He then having received the sop went immediately out: and it was night.

Translation: King James Version

NINA KOSSMAN

Judas' Reproach

(John 13:26–27)

Handing me the bread
dipped in the dish—
not saying.

It was your look.
In your hand:
my shame.

Judas the faithless,
Judas the weak,
eternally.

Forever to regret
not saying
"I will not touch this sop."

JOHN 14:1−2

L et not your heart be troubled: ye believe in God, believe also in me.

2 In my Father's house are many mansions; if it were not so, I would have told you. I go to prepare a place for you.

Translation: King James Version

MARY FULLERTON

Poetry

Ecstatic thought's the thing:
Its nature lifts it from the sod.
The father of its soul is God,
And in God's house are many scansions.

GETHSEMANE

MARK 14:26–42
(Parallel texts: Matthew 26:30–46; Luke 22:39–46; John 18:1–2)

26 And when they had sung a hymn, they went out to the Mount of Olives. [27]And Jesus said to them, "You will all fall away; for it is written, 'I will strike the shepherd, and the sheep will be scattered.' [28]But after I am raised up, I will go before you to Galilee." [29]Peter said to him, "Even though they all fall away, I will not." [30]And Jesus said to him, "Truly, I say to you, this very night, before the cock crows twice, you will deny me three times." [31]But he said vehemently, "If I must die with you, I will not deny you." And they all said the same.

32 And they went to a place which was called Gethsem'ane; and he said to his disciples, "Sit here, while I pray." [33]And he took with him Peter and James and John, and began to be greatly distressed and troubled. [34]And he said to them, "My soul is very sorrowful, even to death; remain here, and watch."[d] [35]And going a little farther, he fell on the ground and prayed that, if it were possible, the hour might pass from him. [36]And he said, "Abba, Father, all things are possible to thee; remove this cup from me; yet not what I will, but what thou wilt." [37]And he came and found them sleeping, and he said to Peter, "Simon, are you asleep? Could you not watch[d] one hour? [38]Watch[d] and pray that you may not enter into temptation; the spirit indeed is willing, but the flesh is weak." [39]And again he went away and prayed, saying the same words. [40]And again he came and found them sleeping, for their eyes were very heavy; and they did not know what to answer him. [41]And he came the third time, and said to them, "Are you still sleeping and

[d] Or keep awake

27: Zech.13.7.

taking your rest? It is enough; the hour has come; the Son of man is betrayed into the hands of sinners. [42]Rise, let us be going; see, my betrayer is at hand."

BORIS PASTERNAK

*Hamlet**

The din quiets. I step onto the boards.
Leaning against the jamb of the door
I try to discern in the distant echo
What will happen in my days.

Through axes of a thousand binoculars
The murk of the night is aimed at me.
If You will, Abba, Father,
Remove this cup from me.

I love your inexorable intent
And I agree to play my part.
But a different drama is on now,
This once, I ask You to spare me.

But the order of acts has been arranged
And the end cannot be forestalled.
I'm alone. All else, sunk to the Pharisee.
To live one's life is no stroll in the park.

Translated from the Russian
by Nina Kossman

*A note on this poem can be found on page 270.

RAINER MARIA RILKE

*The Olive Garden**

He climbed and, under the gray leaves, lost
his gray self in a country of olive trees,
and laid his dusty forehead deep
in the dustiness of his hot hands.

After it all was this. And this the end.
Now I'm to go when I'm becoming blind,
and why is it Your will that I must say
You are, when I find you yourself no more.

Find You no more. Not within me, no.
Not in the others. Not within this rock.
Find You no more. I am alone.

I am alone with all the human grief
I undertook, through You, to soothe,
You, who are not. O shame unnameable . . .

Later they would say: an angel came—.

Why an angel? It was the night that came
leafing through the trees indifferently.
The disciples stirred inside their dreams.
Why an angel? It was the night that came.

The night that came was no uncommon one;
hundreds like it are passing by.
Dogs sleep in them and stones lie down in them.
A melancholy one, one that waits
until, once more, the morning comes.

*A note on this poem can be found on page 270.

For angels answer no such supplicants,
and night is not expansive around them.
All will let go of those who lose themselves,
who are abandoned by the fathers, who
have been excluded from the mother womb.

Translated from the German
by David Curzon and Will Alexander Washburn

PAUL KANE

Disciples Asleep at Gethsemane*

I

I have dreamt a dream of fulfillment, of freedom:
she was an old woman, with a face like the moon,
first full with reflection, then new and dark, and then
we were in a garden and the fountains murmured
words I wanted so much to hear, but mixed suddenly
with harsher tones, with disappointment—a man's voice.
I don't deny it: I hold hard to my needs, myself.

II

Who was I to be chosen? It was late, and I understood
so little—though that little after my own fashion,
and who am I not to be accounted as good as anyone else?
I slept, and in my sleep knew I slept, and dreamed of being
awake—it was enough, surely, for I had been chosen.
Three times he returned and spoke, but I enfolded him
into myself, hearing him say, "Sleep, and take your rest."

*A note on this poem can be found on page 270.

III

There was a meal, a hymn, some wine, and I followed,
wanting to be part of it all. We climbed a hill where
the trees were silver in the darkness, and a wind sighed
about us. It seemed to speak to my heart, saying, "This is
more than you," and so I listened, and followed, knelt
and entered that voice. And then there were lights, a crowd,
confusion, a kiss, and a naked man running away into the dark.

IV

Three times nothing—still nothing, and those
brought to keep faith sleep in the garden.
The master dead, the dream erodes from within,
and sweet hope is made sweeter by perversion:
when it comes down to one, it comes down.
The land is gall—nor milk, nor honey flow,
and false friends keep watch unawake.

RUDYARD KIPLING

Gethsemane

1914–18

The Garden called Gethsemane
    In Picardy it was,
And there the people came to see
    The English soldiers pass.
We used to pass—we used to pass
    Or halt, as it might be,
And ship our masks in case of gas
    Beyond Gethsemane.

The Garden called Gethsemane,
    It held a pretty lass,
But all the time she talked to me
    I prayed my cup might pass.
The officer sat on the chair,
    The men lay on the grass,
And all the time we halted there
    I prayed my cup might pass.

It didn't pass—it didn't pass—
    It didn't pass from me.
I drank it when we met the gas
    Beyond Gethsemane!

JUDAS

MATTHEW 26:47–56
(Parallel texts: Mark 14:43–52; Luke 22:47–53; John 18:3–11)

47 While he was still speaking, Judas came, one of the twelve, and with him a great crowd with swords and clubs, from the chief priests and the elders of the people. ⁴⁸Now the betrayer had given them a sign, saying, "The one I shall kiss is the man; seize him." ⁴⁹And he came up to Jesus at once and said, "Hail, Master!"ⁱ And he kissed him. ⁵⁰Jesus said to him, "Friend, why are you here?"ʲ Then they came up and laid hands on Jesus and seized him. ⁵¹And behold, one of those who were with Jesus stretched out his hand and drew his sword, and struck the slave of the high priest, and cut off his ear. ⁵²Then Jesus said to him, "Put your sword back into its place; for all who take the sword will perish by the sword. ⁵³Do you think that I cannot appeal to my Father, and he will at once send me more than twelve legions of angels? ⁵⁴But how then should the scriptures be fulfilled, that it must be so?" ⁵⁵At that hour Jesus said to the crowds, "Have you come out as against a robber, with swords and clubs to capture me? Day after day I sat in the temple teaching, and you did not seize me. ⁵⁶But all this has taken place, that the scriptures of the prophets might be fulfilled." Then all the disciples forsook him and fled.

ⁱ Or *Rabbi*
ʲ Or *do that for which you have come*

BORIS PASTERNAK

The Garden of Gethsemane

The indifferent glimmer of distant stars
Lit up the turning in the road.
The road went round the Mount of Olives,
Below it streamed the Cedron brook.

The meadow broke off half way.
Beyond, the Milky Way began.
Silver-gray olive trees strained
To walk off into thin air.

At the end was someone's plot of land.
Leaving His disciples outside the wall
He said: "My heart is ready to break
With grief; wait here, keep watch."

He had renounced without struggle
Omnipotence and miracle-working
As though they were borrowed things;
And He became like mortals, like us.

The night's distance seemed on the verge
Of annihilation and nullity.
The range of the universe was uninhabited
And only the garden was a place of life.

And looking into those black chasms,
Void, without beginning or end,
In bloody sweat He implored His Father
To let the cup of death pass Him by.

His mortal anguish quieted by prayer,
He went outside the wall. On the ground
His disciples, overcome with sleep,
Sprawled on the feathergrass of the roadside.

He awakened them: "God granted you
To live in my days, yet you lie there prostrate.
The hour of the Son of Man has struck.
He shall give himself into the hands of sinners."

As soon as He said that from nowhere
A crowd of slaves and tramps appeared.
Swords, torches, and in front of them Judas
With treachery's kiss on his lips.

Peter repulsed the cutthroats with his sword
And cut off the ear of one of them.
But he heard: "Discord is not resolved with metal.
Friend, put your sword back in its place.

Do you think my Father couldn't send
Hosts of winged legions to my help?
And, not touching a single hair on my head,
My enemies would scatter without a trace.

But the book of life has reached a page
More precious than all the holy things.
What was written will now be fulfilled.
Let it be fulfilled then. Amen.

You see, the ages are like a parable,
And in their course they may burst into flame.
In the name of their awesome grandeur
I will go in voluntary torment to my grave.

I will go to my grave and, on the third day, rise,
And just as rafts float down a river
So will the centuries, like barges of a convoy,
Drift toward Me for judgement, from the dark."

Translated from the Russian
by Nina Kossman

WILLIAM BUTLER YEATS

from *"Calvary"*

. . .

Judas [*who has just entered*].   I am Judas.
    That sold you for the thirty pieces of silver.
Christ. You were beside me every day, and saw
    The dead raised up and blind men given their sight,
    And all that I have said and taught you have known,
    Yet doubt that I am God.
Judas.   I have not doubted;
    I knew it from the first moment that I saw you;
    I had no need of miracles to prove it.
Christ. And yet you have betrayed me.
Judas.   I have betrayed you
    Because you seemed all-powerful.
Christ.   My Father
    Even now, if I were but to whisper it,
    Would break the world in His miraculous fury
    To set me free.
Judas.   And is there not one man
    In the wide world that is not in your power?
Christ. My Father put all men into my hands.
Judas. That was the very thought that drove me wild.
    I could not bear to think you had but to whistle
    And I must do; but after that I thought,
    'Whatever man betrays Him will be free';
    And life grew bearable again. And now
    Is there a secret left I do not know,
    Knowing that if a man betrays a God
    He is the stronger of the two?
Christ.   But if
    'Twere the commandment of that God Himself,
    That God were still the stronger.

Judas.   When I planned it
    There was no live thing near me but a heron
    So full of itself that it seemed terrified.
Christ. But my betrayal was decreed that hour
    When the foundations of the world were laid.
Judas. It was decreed that somebody betray you—
    I'd thought of that—but not that I should do it,
    I the man Judas, born on such a day,
    In such a village, such and such his parents;
    Nor that I'd go with my old coat upon me
    To the High Priest, and chuckle to myself
    As people chuckle when alone, and do it.
    For thirty pieces and no more, no less,
    And neither with a nod nor a sent message,
    But with a kiss upon your cheek. I did it,
    I, Judas, and no other man, and now
    You cannot even save me.
Christ.   Begone from me.
    . . .

3 When Judas, his betrayer, saw that he was condemned, he repented and brought back the thirty pieces of silver to the chief priests and the elders, ⁴saying, "I have sinned in betraying innocent blood." They said, "What is that to us? See to it yourself." ⁵And throwing down the pieces of silver in the temple, he departed; and he went and hanged himself. ⁶But the chief priests, taking the pieces of silver, said, "It is not lawful to put them into the treasury, since they are blood money." ⁷So they took counsel, and bought with them the potter's field, to bury strangers in. ⁸Therefore that field has been called the Field of Blood to this day. ⁹Then was fulfilled what had been spoken by the prophet Jeremiah, saying, "And they took the thirty pieces of silver, the price of him on whom a price had been set by some of the sons of Israel, ¹⁰and they gave them for the potter's field, as the Lord directed me."

9–10: Zech.11:12–13; Jer.18:1–3, 32:6–15.

ZBIGNIEW HERBERT

*Hakeldama**

The priests have a problem
on the borderline of ethics and accounting

what to do with the silver coins
Judas threw at their feet

the sum was registered
under the heading of expenses
chroniclers will write it down
under the heading of legend

to record it under the rubic
unexpected earnings would be wrong
to put it in the treasury dangerous
it might infect the silver

it wouldn't be right
to buy a candle holder with it for the temple
or give it to the poor

after long consultation
they decide to buy a potter's field
and build a cemetery
for pilgrims

to give—so to speak
money for death
back to death

the solution
was tactful
therefore why

Hakeldama is Aramaic for "the field of blood."

does the name of this place
rend the air for centuries
Hakeldama
Hakeldama
field of blood

Translated from the Polish
by John and Bogdana Carpenter

JAMES WRIGHT

Saint Judas

When I went out to kill myself, I caught
A pack of hoodlums beating up a man.
Running to spare his suffering, I forgot
My name, my number, how my day began,
How soldiers milled around the garden stone
And sang amusing songs; how all that day
Their javelins measured crowds; how I alone
Bargained the proper coins, and slipped away.

Banished from heaven, I found this victim beaten,
Stripped, kneed, and left to cry. Dropping my rope
Aside, I ran, ignored the uniforms:
Then I remembered bread my flesh had eaten,
The kiss that ate my flesh. Flayed without hope,
I held the man for nothing in my arms.

YEVGENY VINOKUROV

The Mother of Judas

His mother wept so bitterly
As Judas hung from the pine tree.
You should have seen the tears of a mother.
She cried and they could not calm her.
She kissed the blue legs of Judas her son.
Why did these evil people destroy my son?

Translated from the Russian
by Anthony Rudolf

JESUS AND PILATE

MATTHEW 27:11–24
(Parallel texts: Mark 15:1–15; Luke 23:1–25; John 18:29–19:16)

11 Now Jesus stood before the governor; and the governor asked him, "Are you the King of the Jews?" Jesus said, "You have said so." ¹²But when he was accused by the chief priests and elders, he made no answer. ¹³Then Pilate said to him, "Do you not hear how many things they testify against you?" ¹⁴But he gave him no answer, not even to a single charge; so that the governor wondered greatly.

15 Now at the feast the governor was accustomed to release for the crowd any one prisoner whom they wanted. ¹⁶And they had then a notorious prisoner, called Barab′bas.ᵏ ¹⁷So when they had gathered, Pilate said to them, "Whom do you want me to release for you, Barab′basᵏ or Jesus who is called Christ?" ¹⁸For he knew that it was out of envy that they had delivered him up. ¹⁹Besides, while he was sitting on the judgment seat, his wife sent word to him, "Have nothing to do with that righteous man, for I have suffered much over him today in a dream." ²⁰Now the chief priests and the elders persuaded the people to ask for Barab′bas and destroy Jesus. ²¹The governor again said to them, "Which of the two do you want me to release for you?" And they said, "Barab′bas." ²²Pilate said to them, "Then what shall I do with Jesus who is called Christ?" They all said, "Let him be crucified." ²³And he said, "Why, what evil has he done?" But they shouted all the more, "Let him be crucified."

24 So when Pilate saw that he was gaining nothing, but rather

---

ᵏ Other ancient authorities read *Jesus Barabbas*

that a riot was beginning, he took water and washed his hands before the crowd, saying, "I am innocent of this man's blood;[l] see to it yourselves." [25]

RENÉ DAUMAL

Jesus before Pilate

(Matthew, 27)

Jesus before Pilate said nothing. And the governor marvelled greatly. He says to himself: "One does not meet up with this kind of man every day. What pleasure it would have given me to discuss ideas with him, if my official duties did not preclude such things!" He eyes Jesus with longing. But his right hand clasps the knob of the armrest, a reminder of the sphere of the Empire whose faithful and no doubt well-payed official he is. And then, there is Caiaphas, swollen with hatred under his priestly robes, unwilling to let pass this opportunity to unite the skepticism of the Sadducees with the hypocrisy of the Pharisees against the Son of Man. And last of all, there is the mob, calling for Barabbas, that good fellow who already has one foot outside the prison while the carpenters are finishing the cross within. Government, Clergy, Populace: before these three powers, Pilate has only to wash his hands. Everyone here is the prisoner of his office, of his facade, and everyone looks through his mask at the only one who wears no mask, the only one who in fact is one, who looks into the center of his being and sees the living truth: that truth whose name alone so utterly absorbs poor Pontius Pilate.

Translated from the French
by Katharine Washburn

[l] Other authorities read *this righteous blood* or *this righteous man's blood*

24: Dt.21.6–9; Ps.26.6.

DONALD DAVIE

Pilate

The chief of the civil administration
                of the occupying power reflects
in the forty-five minutes he allows himself each morning
over a cigarette for the world to
                re-achieve its third dimension daily
(Saving shadows and memories
                vine on his nerves' snapped trellis):

"Between the judicial and
                the nervously judicious
the best of Rome bleeds
                into the sands of Judaea."

The best? Ho-hum. The keeping up of standards
(The right ones, Roman), how it sustained him once!

The harm it does him,
                the practice of severity
which someone has to do, he
                knows. He knows it. He is bad at it
in his own estimation, but
some one has to and
                whether in good faith
is no problem:
                You keep yourself busy,
too many cases in too little time and such
scruple as there is time for.

Aggressive-pusillanimous, the harm it
did him, and perhaps it does
                any one is known to him, wherein
virtue perhaps. He has
nothing to show to be proud of
                from his H.Q. years but rare

acts of intellectual
                    brutality: "This is no good . . ."
"No, I will not . . ."
                    His
skills were not of that order
                    but being of no account
until perverted, they
                    patiently were perverted:
skills to the end of inspiring
emulation, that
                    ingenious artifice
called "leadership" (and what
an orator he might have been, a
poet even) were
                    perverted to other ends,
to the end of sitting in judgement.

It is the lion of Judah is all claws.
Caiaphas has the style of the officer-class.

Skills to the end of finding
out short-circuited
                    in finding fault, he
knows. He knows it. He is bad at it.

But if it is all he finds with
certainty? The *pax*
Romana is worth something. His
                    wish to be lenient mimes
a charity he dare not
                    not respect but knows he
cannot profess.
                    He does not
in any event perceive
that for these responsible scruples
                    the *soi-disant* King of the Jews
has very much more forbearance
than His accusers.

NINA KOSSMAN

Pilate's Wife

(Matthew 27:19)

I don't know who that man is
but I know when I saw him
my migraine lifted off
like a feather, and some black birds
spelled a message in the air
of my dream, and if you don't
believe in omens, and don't
tell me you do, I know
you don't, they still are there
and since I'm chained to you,
yes, I repeat, I'm chained
to you, you can at least
obey the birds and listen:
Have thou nothing to do
with that just man, husband.

ZBIGNIEW HERBERT

Speculations on the Subject of Barabbas

What happened to Barabbas. I ask no one knows
Released from the chain he walked out into a white
                                        street
he could turn right go straight ahead turn left
spin on his heels crow happily as a rooster
He Emperor of his own hands and head
He Governor of his own breath

I ask because in a sense I took part in the affair
Attracted by the crowd in front of Pilate's palace I
                                        shouted
like the others Barabbas let Barabbas free
Everyone shouted if I alone had been silent
it still would have happened as it was supposed to
                                        happen

Perhaps Barabbas returned to his band
In the mountains he kills quickly robs with precision
Or he opened a pottery shop
And cleans hands soiled by crimes
in the clay of creation
He is a water carrier mule driver money lender
a ship owner—Paul sailed to the Corinthians on one
                                        of them
or—this can't be ruled out—
became a prized spy paid by the Romans

Look and admire the stunning game of fate
for chances of power smiles of fortune

While the Nazarene
remained alone
without an alternative
with a steep
path
of blood

Translated from the Polish
by John and Bogdana Carpenter

THE CRUCIFIXION

LUKE 23:26−38
(Parallel texts: Matthew 27:32−44; Mark 15:21−32; John 19:17−24)

26 And as they led him away, they seized one Simon of Cyre'ne, who was coming in from the country, and laid on him the cross, to carry it behind Jesus. [27]And there followed him a great multitude of the people, and of women who bewailed and lamented him. [28]But Jesus turning to them said, "Daughters of Jerusalem, do not weep for me, but weep for yourselves and for your children. [29]For behold, the days are coming when they will say, 'Blessed are the barren, and the wombs that never bore, and the breasts that never gave suck!' [30]Then they will begin to say to the mountains, 'Fall on us'; and to the hills, 'Cover us.' [31]For if they do this when the wood is green, what will happen when it is dry?"

32 Two others also, who were criminals, were led away to be put to death with him. [33]And when they came to the place which is called The Skull, there they crucified him; and the criminals, one on the right and one on the left. [34]And Jesus said, "Father, forgive them; for they know not what they do."[n] And they cast lots to divide his garments. [35]And the people stood by, watching; but the rulers scoffed at him, saying, "He saved others; let him save himself, if he is the Christ of God, his Chosen One!" [36]The soldiers also mocked him, coming up and offering him vinegar, [37]and saying, "If you are the King of the Jews, save yourself!" [38]There was also an inscription over him,[o] "This is the King of the Jews."

[n] Other ancient authorities omit the sentence *And Jesus . . . what they do*
[o] Other ancient authorities add *in letters of Greek and Latin and Hebrew*

30: Hos.10.8.   31: A proverbial saying which, in this context, probably means: If the innocent Jesus meets such a fate, what will be the fate of the guilty Jerusalem (v. 28)? 34: Num.15.27−31; Ps.22.18.   36: Ps.69.21.

W. H. AUDEN

from *"Horae Canonicae"*

('Immolatus vicerit')

II *Terce*

  After shaking paws with his dog
(Whose bark would tell the world that he is always kind),
  The hangman sets off briskly over the heath;
He does not know yet who will be provided
  To do the high works of Justice with:
Gently closing the door of his wife's bedroom
  (Today she has one of her headaches),
With a sigh the judge descends his marble stair;
  He does not know by what sentence
He will apply on earth the Law that rules the stars:
  And the poet, taking a breather
Round his garden before starting his eclogue,
  Does not know whose Truth he will tell.

  Sprites of hearth and store-room, godlings
Of professional mysteries, the Big Ones
  Who can annihilate a city
Cannot be bothered with this moment: we are left,
  Each to his secret cult. Now each of us
Prays to an image of his image of himself;
  'Let me get through this coming day
Without a dressing down from a superior,
  Being worsted in a repartee,
Or behaving like an ass in front of the girls;
  Let something exciting happen,
Let me find a lucky coin on a sidewalk.
  Let me hear a new funny story.'

  At this hour we all might be anyone:
It is only our victim who is without a wish

Who knows already (that is what
We can never forgive. If he knows the answers,
    Then why are we here, why is there even dust?),
Knows already that, in fact, our prayers are heard,
    That not one of us will slip up,
That the machinery of our world will function
    Without a hitch, that today, for once,
There will be no squabbling on Mount Olympus,
    No Chthonian mutters of unrest,
But no other miracle, knows that by sundown
    We shall have had a good Friday.

EDWIN ARLINGTON ROBINSON

Calvary

Friendless and faint, with martyred steps and slow,
Faint for the flesh, but for the spirit free,
Stung by the mob that came to see the show,
The Master toiled along to Calvary;
We gibed him, as he went, with houndish glee,
Till his dimmed eyes for us did overflow;
We cursed his vengeless hands thrice wretchedly,—
And this was nineteen hundred years ago.

But after nineteen hundred years the shame
Still clings, and we have not made good the loss
That outraged faith has entered in his name.
Ah, when shall come love's courage to be strong!
Tell me, O Lord—tell me, O Lord, how long
Are we to keep Christ writhing on the cross!

ZBIGNIEW HERBERT

The Passion of Our Lord painted by an anonymous hand from the Circle of Rhenish Masters

They have coarse features, their hands are deft and accustomed to a hammer and nails, to wood and iron. Just now they are nailing to the cross Jesus Christ Our Lord. There's lots to be done, they must hurry to get things ready by noon.

Knights on horseback—they are the props of this drama. Impassive faces. Long lances imitate trees without branches on this hillock without trees.

As we said, the fine craftsmen are nailing Our Lord to the cross. Ropes, nails, and a stone for sharpening the tools, are ranged neatly on the sand. There's a hum of activity but without due excitement.

The sand is warm, each grain painstakingly depicted. Here and there a tuft of stiffly erect grass and a marguerite innocently white cheering the eye.

Translated from the Polish
by Adam Czerniawski

HOWARD NEMEROV

from "Gnomes"

A Sacrificed Author
Father, he cried, after the critics' chewing,
Forgive them, for they know not what I'm doing.

39 One of the criminals who were hanged railed at him, saying, "Are you not the Christ? Save yourself and us!" ⁴⁰But the other rebuked him, saying, "Do you not fear God, since you are under the same sentence of condemnation? ⁴¹And we indeed justly; for we are receiving the due reward of our deeds; but this man has done nothing wrong." ⁴²And he said. "Jesus, remember me when you come into ᴾ your kingdom." ⁴³And he said to him, "Truly, I say to you, today you will be with me in Paradise."

ᴾ Other ancient authorities read *in*

JORGE LUIS BORGES

Luke XXIII

Gentile or Hebrew or simply a man
Whose face has been lost in time;
We shall not ransom from oblivion
The silent letters of his name.

He knew of clemency what could
Be known by a petty thief Judea had
Nailed to a cross. Of the preceding time,
We can, today, find nothing. In his final

Task of death by crucifixion,
He heard, among the taunts of the crowd,
That the one who was dying next to him
Was God, and he said, blindly:

Remember me when you come into
Your kingdom, and the inconceivable voice
That will one day be judge of every being
Promised, from the terrible cross,

Paradise. They said nothing more
Until the end, but history
Will not allow the memory to die
Of that afternoon in which these two died.

Oh friends, the innocence of this friend
Of Jesus Christ, the candor that made him
Ask for and be granted Paradise
From the ignominy of punishment

Was what tossed him many times
To sin, to the blood-stained gamble.

Translated from the Spanish
by David Curzon

NICANOR PARRA

The Discourse of the Good Thief

Remember me when thou comest into thy Kingdom
Appoint me President of the Senate
Appoint me Director of the Budget
Appoint me Attorney General of the Republic.

Remember the crown of thorns
Make me Chilean Consul in Stockholm
Appoint me Superintendent of Railroads
Appoint me Commander-in-Chief of the Army.

I'll take anything at all
Administrator of Trustee Territories
Director General of Libraries
Head of the Telegraph and Postal Services.

Head of the Highway Department
Supervisor of Gardens and Parks
Governor of the Province of Ñuble.*

Put me in as Director of the Zoo.

Blessed be the Name of the Father
                And of the Son
                      And of the Holy Spirit
Put me in as Ambassador to any place

---

*Province where the poet was born.

Appoint me Captain of the Colo-Colo Team
Put me in if it pleases you
As President of the Fire-Fighters Union.

Make me Principal of the High School in Ancud.*

If it comes down to it
Put me in as Superintendent of Graveyards.

Translated from the Spanish
by Miller Williams

*Small town in Chile's deep south.

MATTHEW 27:45–56
(Parallel texts: Mark 15:33–41; Luke 23:44–49; John 19:28–37)

45 Now from the sixth hour there was darkness over all the land[m] until the ninth hour. [46]And about the ninth hour Jesus cried with a loud voice, "Eli, Eli, la'ma sabach-tha'ni?" that is, "My God, my God, why hast thou forsaken me?" [47]And some of the bystanders hearing it said, "This man is calling Eli'jah." [48]And one of them at once ran and took a sponge, filled it with vinegar, and put it on a reed, and gave it to him to drink. [49]But the others said, "Wait, let us see whether Eli'jah will come to save him."[n] [50]And Jesus cried again with a loud voice and yielded up his spirit.

51 And behold, the curtain of the temple was torn in two, from top to bottom; and the earth shook, and the rocks were split; [52]the tombs also were opened, and many bodies of the saints who had fallen asleep were raised, [53]and coming out of the tombs after his resurrection they went into the holy city and appeared to many. [54]When the centurion and those who were with him, keeping watch over Jesus, saw the earthquake and what took place, they were filled with awe, and said, "Truly this was the Son[x] of God!"

55 There were also many women there, looking on from afar, who had followed Jesus from Galilee, ministering to him; [56]among whom were Mary Mag'dalene, and Mary the mother of James and Joseph, and the mother of the sons of Zeb'edee.

[m] Or earth
[n] Other ancient authorities insert *And another took a spear and pierced his side, and out came water and blood*
[x] Or *a son*

45: From about noon to about three p.m.   46: *Eli . . . sabachthani,* quoted from Ps.22.1.
47: *Elijah* (similar in sound to *Eli*) was expected to usher in the final period (Mal.4.5–6).
48: Ps.69.21.   51: Ex.26.31–35.

TED HUGHES

A God*

Pain was pulled down over his eyes like a fool's hat.
They pressed electrodes of pain through the parietals.

He was helpless as a lamb
Which cannot be born
Whose head hangs under its mother's anus.

Pain was stabbed through his palm, at the crutch of the M,
Made of iron, from earth's core.
From that pain he hung,
As if he were being weighed.
The cleverness of his fingers availed him
As the bullock's hooves, in the offal bin,
Avail the severed head
Hanging from its galvanized hook.

Pain was hooked through his foot.
From that pain, too, he hung
As on display.
His patience had meaning only for him
Like the sanguine upside-down grin
Of a hanging half-pig.

There, hanging,
He accepted the pain through his ribs
Because he could no more escape it
Than the poulterer's hanging hare,
Hidden behind eyes growing concave,

Can escape
What has replaced its belly.

He could not understand what had happened

Or what he had become.

*A note on this poem can be found on page 270.

ANNA AKHMATOVA

Crucifixion*

"Do not weep for me, Mother,
when I am in my grave."

I

A choir of angels glorified the hour,
the vault of heaven was dissolved in fire.
"Father, why hast Thou forsaken me?
Mother, I beg you, do not weep for me. . . ."

II

Mary Magdalene beat her breasts and sobbed,
His dear disciple, stone-faced, stared.
His mother stood apart. No other looked
into her secret eyes. Nobody dared.

1940–1943

Translated from the Russian
by Stanley Kunitz and Max Hayward

*A note on this poem can be found on page 270.

PAUL CELAN

Tenebrae*

Near are we, Lord,
near and graspable.

Grasped already, Lord,
clawed into each other, as if
each of our bodies were
your body, Lord.

Pray, Lord,
pray to us,
we are near.

Windskewed we went there,
went there, to bend
over pit and crater.

Went to the water-trough, Lord.

It was blood, it was
what you shed, Lord.

It shined.

It cast your image into our eyes, Lord.
Eyes and mouth stand so open and void, Lord.
We have drunk, Lord.
The blood and the image that was in the blood, Lord.

Pray, Lord.
We are near.

Translated from the German
by John Felstiner

*A note on this poem can be found on page 270.

JUDITH WRIGHT

Eli, Eli

To see them go by drowning in the river—
soldiers and elders drowning in the river,
the pitiful women drowning in the river,
the children's faces staring from the river—
that was his cross, and not the cross they gave him.

To hold the invisible wand, and not to save them—
to know them turned to death, and yet not save them;
only to cry to them and not to save them,
knowing that no one but themselves could save them—
this was the wound, more than the wound they dealt him.

To hold out love and know they would not take it,
to hold out faith and know they dared not take it—
the invisible wand, and none would see or take it,
all he could give, and there was none to take it—
thus they betrayed him, not with the tongue's betrayal.

He watched, and they were drowning in the river;
faces like sodden flowers in the river—
faces of children moving in the river;
and all the while, he knew there was no river.

D. H. LAWRENCE

*Eloi, Eloi, Lama Sabachthani?**

How I hate myself, this body which is me;
How it dogs me, what a galling shadow!
How I would like to cut off my hands,
And take out my intestines to torture them!

But I can't, for it is written against me I must not,
I must preserve my life from hurt.

But then, that shadow's shadow of me,
The enemy!

God, how glad I am to hear the shells
Droning over, threatening me!
It is their threat, their loud, jeering threat,
Like screaming birds of Fate
Wheeling to lacerate and rip up this my body,
It is the loud cries of these birds of pain
That gives me peace.

For I hate this body, which is so dear to me:
My legs, my breast, my belly:
My God, what agony they are to me;
For I dote on them with tenderness, and I hate them,
I hate them bitterly.

My God, that they should always be with me!
Nay, now at last thank God for the jeopardy,
For the shells, that the question is now no more before me.

I do not die, I am not even hurt,
But I kill my shadow's shadow of me!
And God is good, yes, God is very good!
I shot my man, I saw him crumble and hang
A moment as he fell—and grovel, and die.

*A note on this poem can be found on page 270.

And God is good, for I wanted him to die,
To twist, and grovel, and become a heap of dirt
In death. This death, his death, my death—
It is the same, this death.

So when I run at length thither across
To the trenches, I see again a face with blue eyes,
A blanched face, fixed and agonized,
Waiting. And I knew he wanted it.
Like a bride he took my bayonet, wanting it,
Like a virgin the blade of my bayonet, wanting it,
And it sank to rest from me in him,
And I, the lover, am consummate,
And he is the bride, I have sown him with the seed
And planted and fertilized him.

But what are you, woman, peering through the rents
In the purple veil?
Would you peep in the empty house like a pilferer?
You are mistaken, the veil of the flesh is rent
For the Lord to come forth at large, on the scent of blood,
Not for the thieves to enter, the pilferers.

Is there no reconciliation?
Is marriage only with death?
In death the consummation?
What I beget, must I beget of blood?
Are the guns and the steel the bridegroom,
Our flesh the bride?

I had dreamed of love, oh love, I had dreamed of love,
And the veil of the temple rent at the kiss on kiss.
And God revealed through the sweat and the heat of love,
And God abroad and alight on us everywhere,
Everywhere men and women alight with God,
My body glad as the bell of a flower
And hers a flowerbell swinging
In a breeze of knowledge.

Why should we hate, then, with this hate incarnate?
Why am I bridegroom of War, war's paramour?
What is the crime, that my seed is turned to blood,
My kiss to wounds?
Who is it will have it so, who did the crime?
And why do the women follow us satisfied,
Feed on our wounds like bread, receive our blood
Like glittering seed upon them for fulfilment?

Lord, what we have done we hereby expiate,
We expiate in our bodies' rents and rags
In our sheaf of self-gathered wounds: we go to meet
Our bride among the rustling chorus of shells,
Whose birds they are,
We give up, O Lord, our bodies to deadly hate,
We take the bride, O God, and our seed of life
Runs richly from us.
We expiate it thus, the unknowable crime,
We give hate her dues, O God, we yield her up
Our bodies to the expiation, Lord.

But shall I touch hands with death in killing that other,
The enemy, my brother?
Shall I offer to him my brotherly body to kill,
Be bridegroom or best man, as the case turns out?

The odds are even, and he will have it so.
It may be I shall give the bride
And the marriage shall be my brother's—it may be so—
I walk the earth intact hereafterwards;
The crime full-expiate, the Erinnyes sunk
Like blood in the earth again; we walk the earth
Unchallenged, intact, unabridged, henceforth a host
Cleansed and in concord from the bed of death.

EDWIN MUIR

The Killing

That was the day they killed the Son of God
On a squat hill-top by Jerusalem.
Zion was bare, her children from their maze
Sucked by the demon curiosity
Clean through the gates. The very halt and blind
Had somehow got themselves up to the hill.

After the ceremonial preparation,
The scourging, nailing, nailing against the wood,
Erection of the main-trees with their burden,
While from the hill rose an orchestral wailing,
They were there at last, high up in the soft spring day.
We watched the writhings, heard the moanings, saw
The three heads turning on their separate axles
Like broken wheels left spinning. Round *his* head
Was loosely bound a crown of plaited thorn
That hurt at random, stinging temple and brow
As the pain swung into its envious circle.
In front the wreath was gathered in a knot
That as he gazed looked like the last stump left
Of a death-wounded deer's great antlers. Some
Who came to stare grew silent as they looked,
Indignant or sorry. But the hardened old
And the hard-hearted young, although at odds
From the first morning, cursed him with one curse,
Having prayed for a Rabbi or an armed Messiah
And found the Son of God. What use to them
Was a God or a Son of God? Of what avail
For purposes such as theirs? Beside the cross-foot,
Alone, four women stood and did not move
All day. The sun revolved, the shadow wheeled,
The evening fell. His head lay on his breast,

But in his breast they watched his heart move on
By itself alone, accomplishing its journey.
Their taunts grew louder, sharpened by the knowledge

That he was walking in the park of death,
Far from their rage. Yet all grew stale at last,
Spite, curiosity, envy, hate itself.
They waited only for death and death was slow
And came so quietly they scarce could mark it.
They were angry then with death and death's deceit.

I was a stranger, could not read these people
Or this outlandish deity. Did a God
Indeed in dying cross my life that day
By chance, he on his road and I on mine?

SALVATORE QUASIMODO

Anno Domini MCMXLVII

You have stopped beating the drums
with a dying fall on all horizons
behind flag-draped coffins, stopped
giving up wounds and tears to pity
in the razed cities, ruin on ruin.
And no one cries any longer "O God why hast
thou forsaken me?" No milk
nor blood flows any more from the riddled breast.
Now you have hidden the guns among the magnolias,
leave us one day without arms, on the grass
with the sound of moving water
and fresh leaves of cane in our hair
while we clasp the woman who loves us.
At nightfall sound no sudden
curfew. A day, a single
day for ourselves, O lords of the earth,
before once again air and metal heave
and a splinter catches us full in the face.

Translated from the Italian
by Jack Bevan

ZBIGNIEW HERBERT

Meditations of Mr. Cogito on Redemption

He should not have sent his son

too many have seen
his son's pierced hands
his ordinary skin

> it was written
> to reconcile us
> by the worst reconciliation

too many nostrils
have breathed with delight
the odor of his fear

> one should not descend
> low
> fraternize with blood

he should not have sent his son
it was better to reign
in a baroque palace made out of marble clouds
on a throne of terror
with a scepter of death

Translated from the Polish
by John and Bogdana Carpenter

DICK BARNES

Chuang Tzu and Hui Tzu*

Chuang Tzu and Hui Tzu were hundreds of years old.
They flew over Galilee. Hui Tzu said,
"There goes another country boy."
"Country boy my ass," said Chuang Tzu,
"you just watch him crucifly away
up to the sky." Hui Tzu said, "You mean
crucify, not crucifly: crucify,
you asshole." Chuang Tzu said,
"Excuse me if you are mistaken."

WILFRED OWEN

At a Calvary near the Ancre†

One ever hangs where shelled roads part.
    In this war He too lost a limb,
But His disciples hide apart;
    And now the Soldiers bear with Him.

Near Golgotha strolls many a priest,
    And in their faces there is pride
That they were flesh-marked by the Beast
    By whom the gentle Christ's denied.

The scribes on all the people shove
    And brawl allegiance to the state,
But they who love the greater love
    Lay down their life; they do not hate.

*A note on this poem can be found on page 270.
†A note on this poem can be found on page 271.

J. KATES

No Altarpiece*

No altarpiece includes the painter
fronting the scene
from whom the weeping mother
turns, John shielding her
like a gangster's hat
from his quick eye.

He props his easel as the cross is set,
readies his first deft strokes,
half hearing cries and registering their effect
unmoved among the crowd
before the light fails.

Later in the studio details
can be fleshed out,
colors deepened, the perspective
of the thieves perfected,
qualities adjusted.

*A note on this poem can be found on page 271.

DANIEL WEISSBORT

Mourning*

It's not that you were present,
but that suddenly I knew how it was done.
The broken piano, standing in the empty room—
I pictured you seated there.
And I sang: *Eli, Eli* . . .
And my voice even broke,
mimicking yours in old age.

Remembering you acting that part,
however petulantly,
is to evoke your aspirations,
your despair as well.
It is to open the ear to those distinct vibrations,
for an instant to be filled with you,
and nothing else.

*A note on this poem can be found on page 271.

THOMAS HARDY

Unkept Good Fridays

There are many more Good Fridays
 Than this, if we but knew
The names, and could relate them,
 Of men whom rulers slew
For their goodwill, and date them
 As runs the twelvemonth through.

These nameless Christs' Good Fridays,
 Whose virtues wrought their end,
Bore days of bonds and burning,
 With no man to their friend,
Of mockeries, and spurning;
 Yet they are all unpenned.

When they had their Good Fridays
 Of bloody sweat and strain
Oblivion hides. We quote not
 Their dying words of pain,
Their sepulchres we note not,
 Unwitting where they have lain.

No annual Good Fridays
 Gained they from cross and cord,
From being sawn asunder,
 Disfigured and abhorred,
Smitten and trampled under:
 Such dates no hands have scored.

Let be. Let lack Good Fridays
 These Christs of unwrit names;
The world was not even worthy
 To taunt their hopes and aims,
As little of earth, earthy,
 As his mankind proclaims.

Good Friday, 1927

JÁNOS PILINSZKY

Passion of Ravensbrück

He steps out from the others.
He stands in the square silence.
The prison garb, the convict's skull
blink like a projection.

He is horribly alone.
His pores are visible.
Everything about him is so gigantic,
everything is so tiny.

And this is all.
         The rest—
the rest was simply
that he forgot to cry out
before he collapsed.

Translated from the Hungarian
by János Csokits and Ted Hughes

ANNA KAMIENSKA

On the Cross*

He was dying on the cross
on a hospital bed
loneliness stood there by his side
the mother of sorrows

Lips closed
and feet tied
My God my God
why have you forsaken me

Sudden silence
All had happened
that was to happen
between someone
and God

8 May 1986

Translated from the Polish
by David Curzon and Grażyna Drabik

*A note on this poem can be found on page 271.

THE DEPOSITION

MATTHEW 27:57–61
(Parallel texts: Mark 15:42–47; Luke 23:50–56; John 19:38–42)

57 When it was evening, there came a rich man from Arimathe′a, named Joseph, who also was a disciple of Jesus. ⁵⁸He went to Pilate and asked for the body of Jesus. Then Pilate ordered it to be given to him. ⁵⁹And Joseph took the body, and wrapped it in a clean linen shroud, ⁶⁰and laid it in his own new tomb, which he had hewn in the rock; and he rolled a great stone to the door of the tomb, and departed. ⁶¹Mary Mag′dalene and the other Mary were there, sitting opposite the sepulchre.

RAINER MARIA RILKE

Pietà

And so, Jesus, I see your feet again
that were a young man's feet when I,
trembling, uncovered them and washed them down;
and how they stood, entangled in my hair,
like some white wildebeest half in a thornbush.

I see, like this, your limbs that were not loved
for the first time in this, our night of love.
At last you fill my arms and I'm
in admiration, watching over you.

But look, your hands are torn—:
not from love-bites, my darling, not from me.
Your heart lies open for any to go in:
it should have been an entrance that was mine.

Now you are tired, and your tired mouth
has no desire for my own aching mouth—.
O Jesus, Jesus, which hour belonged to us?
How strangely both of us are foundering.

Translated from the German
by David Curzon and Will Alexander Washburn

BORIS PASTERNAK

Magdalene (I)

With the night, my demon appears,
The price I pay for my past.
They come and gnaw at my heart,
Those memories of vice
When I, a slave to male whims,
Was a frenzied fool
And the street was my home.

A few minutes are left,
Then a quiet like the grave will fall
But before they pass, I,
At the limit of my life,
Will shatter it, like a vessel
Of alabaster, in front of You.

Oh, where would I be now,
My Teacher and my Saviour,
If Eternity weren't waiting for me
In the nights, at the table,
Like a new guest enticed
Into the net of my trade.

But explain to me the meaning
Of sin, death, hell, brimstone,
When, in sight of all, I have grown
One with You, a vine and its tree,
In my yearning that has no bound.

When, Jesus, I clasp Your feet,
Supporting them on my knees,
Perhaps I'm learning to embrace
The squared beam of the cross,
In a trance, straining for Your body,
As I prepare You for burial.

Translated from the Russian by Nina Kossman

MARINA TSVETAYEVA

Magdalene

I

Ten commandments are between us:
The heat of ten bonfires.
Kindred blood recoils,
For me you are foreign blood.

In the times of the Gospels
I would have been one of those . . .
(Foreign blood is the most desirable
And most foreign of all!)

With all my weaknesses,
I would be drawn to you, stretching out to you—
A bright color! Hiding
With demonic eyes, I would pour oils

Onto your feet, and under them,
And simply, into the sands . . .
Passion sold among the merchants,
It is spit out—flow!

With the foam of lips and crusts
Of eyes and with the sweat of all
Bliss . . . In my hair I wrap
Your feet, as though in fur.

I spread like a fabric
Under your feet . . . It is not he (she!)
Who spake to a creature
With fiery curls: arise, sister!

August 26

II

Ointments bought for three times
Their value, the sweat of passion,
Tears, hair,—a total
Flowing out, but that one

Fixed his blessed gaze
Into a dry red clay:
—Magdalene! Magdalene!
Do not give so much of yourself!

August 31

III

I will not ask about your paths,
Dear one!—for all has come to pass.
I was barefoot, and you put shoes on me
With downpours of hair—
And—tears.

I will not ask you at what price
These oils were bought.
I was naked, and you enclosed me
With the wave of your body
Like a wall.

I will touch your nakedness with fingers
More quietly than waters, more softly than grass.
I was upright, and you taught me to bow
With tenderness, lowering yourself before me.

In your hair dig out a hole for me,
Swathe me without linen.
—Carrier of myrrh! Why do I need chrism?
You washed me all over
Like a wave.

August 31

Translated from the Russian
by Michael M. Naydan and Slava Yastremski

236 | *The Gospels in Our Image*

LAWRENCE FERLINGHETTI

Christ Climbed Down

Christ climbed down
from His bare Tree
this year
and ran away to where
there were no rootless Christmas trees
hung with candycanes and breakable stars

Christ climbed down
from His bare Tree
this year
and ran away to where
there were no gilded Christmas trees
and no tinsel Christmas trees
and no tinfoil Christmas trees
and no pink plastic Christmas trees
and no gold Christmas trees
and no black Christmas trees
and no powderblue Christmas trees
hung with electric candles
and encircled by tin electric trains
and clever cornball relatives

Christ climbed down
from His bare Tree
this year
and ran away to where
no intrepid Bible salesmen
covered the territory
in two-tone cadillacs
and where no Sears Roebuck creches
complete with plastic babe in manger
arrived by parcel post
the babe by special delivery

and where no televised Wise Men
praised the Lord Calvert Whiskey

Christ climbed down
from His bare Tree
this year
and ran away to where
no fat handshaking stranger
in a red flannel suit
and a fake white beard
went around passing himself off
as some sort of North Pole saint
crossing the desert to Bethlehem
Pennsylvania
in a Volkswagen sled
drawn by rollicking Adirondack reindeer
with German names
and bearing sacks of Humble Gifts
from Saks Fifth Avenue
for everybody's imagined Christ child

Christ climbed down
from His bare Tree
this year
and ran away to where
no Bing Crosby carollers
groaned of a tight Christmas
and where no Radio City angels
iceskated wingless
thru a winter wonderland
into a jinglebell heaven
daily at 8:30
with Midnight Mass matinees

Christ climbed down
from His bare Tree
this year
and softly stole away into
some anonymous Mary's womb again
where in the darkest night
of everybody's anonymous soul
He awaits again
an unimaginable
and impossibly
Immaculate Reconception
the very craziest
of Second Comings

THE EMPTY TOMB

MATTHEW 28:1–6
(Parallel texts: Mark 16:1–8; Luke 24:1–12; John 20:1–2)

28 Now after the sabbath, toward the dawn of the first day of the week, Mary Mag′dalene and the other Mary went to see the sepulchre. ²And behold, there was a great earthquake; for an angel of the Lord descended from heaven and came and rolled back the stone, and sat upon it. ³His appearance was like lightning, and his raiment white as snow. ⁴And for fear of him the guards trembled and became like dead men. ⁵But the angel said to the women, "Do not be afraid; for I know that you seek Jesus who was crucified. ⁶He is not here; for he has risen, as he said. Come, see the place where heq lay.["]

---

q Other ancient authorities read *the Lord*

CZESLAW MILOSZ

from *"Six Lectures in Verse"*

Lecture V

"Christ has risen." Whoever believes that
Should not behave as we do,
Who have lost the up, the down, the right, the left, heavens,
    abysses,
And try somehow to muddle on, in cars, in beds,
Men clutching at women, women clutching at men,
Falling, rising, putting coffee on the table,
Buttering bread, for here's another day.

And another year. Time to exchange presents.
Christmas trees aglow, music,
All of us, Presbyterians, Lutherans, Catholics,
Like to sit in the pew, sing with others,
Give thanks for being here together still,
For the gift of echoing the Word, now and in all ages.

We rejoice at having been spared the misfortune
Of countries where, as we read, the enslaved
Kneel before the idol of the State, live and die with its name
On their lips, not knowing they're enslaved.
However that may be, The Book is always with us,
And in it, miraculous signs, counsels, orders.
Unhygienic, it's true, and contrary to common sense,
But they exist and that's enough on the mute earth.
It's as if a fire warmed us in a cave
While outside the golden rain of stars is motionless.
Theologians are silent. And philosophers
Don't even dare ask: "What is truth?"
And so, after the great wars, undecided,
With almost good will but not quite,
We plod on with hope. And now let everyone
Confess to himself. "Has he risen?" "I don't know."

Translated from the Polish by Czeslaw Milosz and Leonard Nathan

THE RESURRECTION

JOHN 20:11–18
(Parallel text: Mark 16:9–11)

11 But Mary stood weeping outside the tomb, and as she wept she stooped to look into the tomb; ¹²and she saw two angels in white, sitting where the body of Jesus had lain, one at the head and one at the feet. ¹³They said to her, "Woman, why are you weeping?" She said to them, "Because they have taken away my Lord, and I do not know where they have laid him." ¹⁴Saying this, she turned round and saw Jesus standing, but she did not know that it was Jesus. ¹⁵Jesus said to her, "Woman, why are you weeping? Whom do you seek?" Supposing him to be the gardener, she said to him, "Sir, if you have carried him away, tell me where you have laid him, and I will take him away." ¹⁶Jesus said to her, "Mary." She turned and said to him in Hebrew, "Rab-bo′ni!" (which means Teacher). ¹⁷Jesus said to her, "Do not hold me, for I have not yet ascended to the Father; but go to my brethren and say to them, I am ascending to my Father and your Father, to my God and your God." ¹⁸Mary Mag′dalene went and said to the disciples, "I have seen the Lord"; and she told them that he had said these things to her.

RAINER MARIA RILKE

Mary at Peace with the Risen Lord

What they felt then: isn't it
sweeter than every secret,
than all that's only earth:
when he, still pale from the grave,
came assuaged to her:
in all ways resurrected.
O to her first. And they were then
being saved, ineffably.
Yes, being saved, that's it. They had no need
to touch each other firmly.
He laid for a second—
if that—his soon to be
eternal hand on her woman's shoulder.
And they began,
at peace, like trees in Spring,
the boundless and the bounded,
the season of this
their utmost association.

Translated from the German
by David Curzon and Will Alexander Washburn

13 That very day two of them were going to a village named Emma'us, about seven miles[w] from Jerusalem, [14]and talking with each other about all these things that had happened. [15]While they were talking and discussing together, Jesus himself drew near and went with them. [16]But their eyes were kept from recognizing him. [17]And he said to them, "What is this conversation which you are holding with each other as you walk?" And they stood still, looking sad. [18]Then one of them, named Cle'opas, answered him, "Are you the only visitor to Jerusalem who does not know the things that have happened there in these days?" [19]And he said to them, "What things?" And they said to him, "Concerning Jesus of Nazareth, who was a prophet mighty in deed and word before God and all the people, [20]and how our chief priests and rulers delivered him up to be condemned to death, and crucified him. [21]But we had hoped that he was the one to redeem Israel. Yes, and besides all this, it is now the third day since this happened. [22]Moreover, some women of our company amazed us. They were at the tomb early in the morning [23]and did not find his body; and they came back saying that they had even seen a vision of angels, who said that he was alive. [24]Some of those who were with us went to the tomb, and found it just as the women had said; but him they did not see." [25]And he said to them, "O foolish men, and slow of heart to believe all that the prophets have spoken! [26]Was it not necessary that the Christ should suffer these things and enter into his glory?" [27]And beginning with Moses and all the prophets, he interpreted to them in all the scriptures the things concerning himself.

28 So they drew near to the village to which they were going. He appeared to be going further, [29]but they constrained him,

[w] Greek *sixty stadia;* some ancient authorities read *a hundred and sixty stadia*

saying, "Stay with us, for it is toward evening and the day is now far spent." So he went in to stay with them. ³⁰When he was at table with them, he took the bread and blessed, and broke it, and gave it to them. ³¹And their eyes were opened and they recognized him; and he vanished out of their sight. ³²They said to each other, "Did not our hearts burn within us᷍ while he talked to us on the road, while he opened to us the scriptures?"

᷍ Other ancient authorities omit *within us*

ERIC PANKEY

The Confession of Cleopas

The spice and pungent air of the earth,
Rising from where they had sealed it,

From where they had placed a treasure,
Chilled me with its damp impoverishment.

Only hearsay and my slow heart
Kept me company. I doubted

And when I looked there was nothing,
Not even shadows or enigma.

I thought evidence would stack up
Like so many bricks in an archway,

That some final event would wedge
The keystone in and hold.

How could I know the moment I moved
Within except in retrospect?

LUKE 24:36–49

(Parallel texts: Matthew 28:16–20; Mark 16:12–18; John 20:19–23)

36 As they were saying this, Jesus himself stood among them.ˣ
³⁷But they were startled and frightened, and supposed that they
saw a spirit. ³⁸And he said to them, "Why are you troubled, and
why do questionings rise in your hearts? ³⁹See my hands and my
feet, that it is I myself; handle me, and see; for a spirit has not flesh
and bones as you see that I have."ʸ ⁴¹And while they still disbelieved
for joy, and wondered, he said to them, "Have you anything here
to eat?" ⁴²They gave him a piece of broiled fish, ⁴³and he took it and
ate before them.

44 Then he said to them, "These are my words which I spoke
to you, while I was still with you, that everything written about me
in the law of Moses and the prophets and the psalms must be ful-
filled." ⁴⁵Then he opened their minds to understand the scriptures,
⁴⁶and said to them, "Thus it is written, that the Christ should suffer
and on the third day rise from the dead, ⁴⁷and that repentance and
forgiveness of sins should be preached in his name to all nations,ᶻ
beginning from Jerusalem. ⁴⁸You are witnesses of these things.
⁴⁹And behold, I send the promise of my Father upon you; but stay
in the city, until you are clothed with power from on high."

ˣ Other ancient authorities add *and said to them, "Peace to you!"*
ʸ Other ancient authorities add verse 40, *And when he had said this, he showed them his hands and his
feet*
ᶻ Or *nations. Beginning from Jerusalem you are witnesses*

46: Hos.6.2.

A. D. HOPE

Easter Hymn

Make no mistake; there will be no forgiveness;
No voice can harm you and no hand will save;
Fenced by the magic of deliberate darkness
You walk on the sharp edges of the wave;

Trouble with soul again the putrefaction
Where Lazarus three days rotten lies content.
Your human tears will be the seed of faction,
Murder the sequel to your sacrament.

The City of God is built like other cities:
Judas negotiates the loans you float;
You will meet Caiaphas upon committees;
You will be glad of Pilate's casting vote.

Your truest lovers still the foolish virgins,
Your heart will sicken at the marriage feasts
Knowing they watch you from the darkened gardens
Being polite to your official guests.

MARK 16:19−20
(Parallel text: Luke 24:50−53)

19 So then the Lord Jesus, after he had spoken to them, was taken up into heaven, and sat down at the right hand of God. ²⁰And they went forth and preached everywhere, while the Lord worked with them and confirmed the message by the signs that attended it. Amen.

A. E. HOUSMAN

Easter Hymn

If in that Syrian garden, ages slain,
You sleep, and know not you are dead in vain,
Nor even in dreams behold how dark and bright
Ascends in smoke and fire by day and night
The hate you died to quench and could but fan,
Sleep well and see no morning, son of man.

But if, the grave rent and the stone rolled by,
At the right hand of majesty on high
You sit, and sitting so remember yet
Your tears, your agony and bloody sweat,
Your cross and passion and the life you gave,
Bow hither out of heaven and see and save.

MATTHEW 28:16−20

16 Now the eleven disciples went to Galilee, to the mountain to which Jesus had directed them. ¹⁷And when they saw him they worshiped him; but some doubted. ¹⁸And Jesus came and said to them, "All authority in heaven and on earth has been given to me. ¹⁹Go therefore and make disciples of all nations, baptizing them in the name of the Father and of the Son and of the Holy Spirit, ²⁰teaching them to observe all that I have commanded you; and lo, I am with you always, to the close of the age."

WILLIAM BUTLER YEATS

from *"Two Songs from a Play"*⋆

II

In pity for man's darkening thought
He walked that room and issued thence
In Galilean turbulence;
The Babylonian starlight brought
A fabulous, formless darkness in;
Odour of blood when Christ was slain
Made all Platonic tolerance vain
And vain all Doric discipline.

Everything that man esteems
Endures a moment or a day.
Love's pleasure drives his love away,
The painter's brush consumes his dreams;
The herald's cry, the soldier's tread
Exhaust his glory and his might:
Whatever flames upon the night
Man's own resinous heart has fed.

⋆A note on this poem can be found on page 271.

THE WORD MADE FLESH

JOHN 1:1 and 14

1 In the beginning was the Word, and the Word was with God, and the Word was God.

. . .

14 And the Word became flesh and dwelt among us, full of grace and truth; we have beheld his glory, glory as of the only Son from the Father.

GAIL HOLST-WARHAFT

In the End Is the Body

In the end is the body—what we know
as inspiration departs before
the final assault of pain and decay.
Even the carpenter's son from Nazareth
could not, in the end, overcome
the body's claims though he knew
inspiration more than most.

And don't imagine his mother
was indifferent to the hammer smashing
the arrangement of bone and sinew she
had held in hers at his beginning.
She wished him back unpierced, smelling
of sawdust and sweat. He was the one
she'd hoped would close her eyes in the end.

In the end my mother lay
body-bound, curled like a foetus,
fretting for a peppermint, a sip of whiskey,
the pillow turned this way and that,
and she a woman who, buoyant in silk
and shingled hair, stood on the hill
at Fiesole reciting her Browning to the wind.

JORGE LUIS BORGES

John 1:14 (1969)

This page will be no less a riddle
than those of My holy books
or those others repeated
by ignorant mouths
believing them the handiwork of a man,
not the Spirit's dark mirrors.
I who am the Was, the Is, and the Is To Come
again condescend to the written word,
which is time in succession and no more than an emblem.

Who plays with a child plays with something
near and mysterious;
wanting once to play with My children,
I stood among them with awe and tenderness.
I was born of a womb
by an act of magic.
I lived under a spell, imprisoned in a body,
in the humbleness of a soul.
I knew memory,
that coin that's never twice the same.
I knew hope and fear,
those twin faces of the uncertain future.
I knew wakefulness, sleep, dreams,
ignorance, the flesh,
reason's roundabout labyrinths,
the friendship of men,
the blind devotion of dogs.
I was loved, understood, praised, and hung from a cross.
I drank My cup to the dregs.
My eyes saw what they had never seen—
night and its many stars.
I knew things smooth and gritty, uneven and rough,

the taste of honey and apple,
water in the throat of thirst,
the weight of metal in the hand,
the human voice, the sound of footsteps on the grass,
the smell of rain in Galilee,
the cry of birds on high.
I knew bitterness as well.
I have entrusted the writing of these words to a common man;
they will never be what I want to say
but only their shadow.
These signs are dropped from My eternity.
Let someone else write the poem, not he who is now its scribe.
Tomorrow I shall be a great tree in Asia,
or a tiger among tigers
preaching My law to the tiger's woods.
Sometimes homesick, I think back
on the smell of that carpenter's shop.

Translated from the Spanish
by Norman Thomas di Giovanni

ACKNOWLEDGMENTS

Jeffrey Fiskin, whose judgments I trusted more than my own and sought for every choice and on all drafts; and others who have given advice, suggestions, corrections, and information, and sustained my belief in the project: Stanley H. Barkan, Deborah Brodie, Lynne Bundesen, Maurice Clapisson, Paul E. Dinter, Bert Gross, Linda Gutstein, Ya'acov Hanoch, Susan Kinsolving, Jesse Rosenthal, Lori Seibel, Burton L. Visotzky, Gail Holst-Warhaft, Zellman Warhaft. The anthology was started in The Writers Room, the urban writers' retreat in Greenwich Village. Sharon Friedman of John Hawkins & Associates was my guide and protector in the world of publishing. Ruth Greenstein of Harcourt Brace was my advocate and editor.

PERMISSIONS

Gospels texts are from the *Revised Standard Version of the Bible,* copyright 1946, 1952, 1971 by the Division of Christian Education of the National Council of Churches of Christ in the USA. Used by permission.

Annotations to passages from the Gospels are from *The Oxford Annotated Bible,* edited by Herbert G. May and Bruce M. Metzger. Copyright © 1962, 1990 by Oxford University Press, Inc. Reprinted by permission.

Akhmatova, Anna: "Crucifixion" is translated by Stanley Kunitz and Max Hayward. Reprinted by permission of Darhansoff & Verrill Literary Agency.

Appleman, Philip: "Mary" is from *Let There Be Light.* Reprinted courtesy of Bantam Doubleday Dell.

Auden, W. H.: The excerpt from "The Prolific and the Devourer" is reprinted by permission of The Ecco Press. "II Terce," excerpted from "Horae Canonicae," is from *Collected Poems.* Copyright © 1955 by W. H. Auden. Reprinted by permission of Random House, Inc.

Barańczak, Stanisław: "N. N. Tries to Remember the Words of a Prayer," translated by Kevin Windle, is reprinted by permission. "The Three Magi" is reprinted by permission of the author, the translator, and TriQuarterly Books, Northwestern University.

Barnes, Dick: "Chuang Tzu and Hui Tzu" is used by permission of the author.

Bishop, Elizabeth: "The Prodigal" is from *The Complete Poems, 1927–1979.* Copyright © 1979, 1983 by Alice Helen Methfessel. Reprinted by permission of Farrar, Straus & Giroux, Inc.

Borges, Jorge Luis: "From an Apocryphal Gospel" and "John 1:14" are from *In Praise of Darkness,* translated by Norma Thomas di Giovanni. Translation copyright © 1969, 1970, 1971, 1972, 1973, 1974 by Emece Editores, S.A., and Norman Thomas di Giovanni. Reprinted by permission of Dutton Signet, a division of Penguin Books USA Inc. "John 1:14 (1964)," translation copyright © 1995 by David Curzon and Sarah Recalde, and "Luke XXIII" and "Matthew XXV:30," translation copyright © 1995 by David Curzon, are from *The Collected Works of Jorge Luis Borges.* Reprinted by permission of Viking Penguin, a division of Penguin Books USA Inc.

Brecht, Bertolt: "Mary" is from *Poems 1913–1956.* Reprinted by permission of Reed Consumer Books.

Bunin, Ivan: "Flowers, and tall-stalked grasses, and a bee" is translated by David Curzon and Vladislav I. Guerassev. Reprinted by permission of the translators.

Cardenal, Ernesto: "Unrighteous Mammon (Luke 16:9)" is from *Apocalypse and*

Hughes. Reprinted by permission of HarperCollins Publishers, Inc. and Faber and Faber Ltd.

Iman, Yusef: "Love Your Enemy" is used by permission of Amiri Baraka.

Jammes, Francis: "The Five Sorrowful Mysteries" is translated by Jeffrey Fiskin. Reprinted by permission of the translator.

Kamienska, Anna: "Annunciation," "Those Who Carry," "Saint Martha," "Things of This World" and "On the Cross" are translated by Grażyna Drabik and David Curzon. Reprinted by permission of Daniel Weissbort, editor, *Modern Poetry in Translation,* and the translators.

Kane, Paul: "Disciples Asleep at Gethsemane" is used by permission of the author.

Kates, J.: "No Altarpiece" was previously published in *Arion's Dolphin.* Reprinted by permission of the author.

Kipling, Rudyard: "A Nativity," "The Sons of Martha," and "Gethsemane" are from *Rudyard Kipling's Verse: Definitive Edition.* Reprinted courtesy of Bantam Doubleday Dell.

Kirchwey, Karl: "He Considers the Birds of the Air" originally appeared in the *New Yorker.* Copyright © 1994 Karl Kirchwey. Reprinted by permission.

Kossman, Nina: "Judas' Reproach" and "Pilate's Wife" are reprinted by permission of the author.

Larkin, Philip: "Faith Healing" is from *Collected Poems.* Copyright © 1988, 1989 by the Estate of Phillip Larkin. Reprinted by permission of Farrar, Straus & Giroux, Inc. and Faber and Faber Inc.

Lawrence, D. H.: "Demiurge," "Commandments," "Lord's Prayer," and "Eloi, Eloi, Lama Sabachthani?" are from *The Complete Poems of D. H. Lawrence,* edited by V. de Sola Pinto and F. W. Roberts. Copyright © 1964, 1971 by Angelo Ravagli and C. M. Weekley, Executors of the Estate of Frieda Lawrence Ravagli. Reprinted by permission of Viking Penguin, a division of Penguin Books USA Inc., and Lawrence Pollinger Ltd.

Levi, Primo: "Annunciation" is from *Collected Poems.* English translation copyright © 1984 by Ruth Feldman. Reprinted by permission of Faber and Faber, Inc.

Machado, Antonio: "Lord, You Have Ripped Away" is from *Times Alone: Selected Poems of Antonio Machado,* translated by Robert Bly and published by Wesleyan University Press. Copyright © 1983 by Robert Bly. Reprinted by permission of the translator.

Maksimović, Desanka: "For the Barren Woman," translated from the Serbo-Croatian by Ivo Soljan, is from *Lips #17: International Women Poets Anthology #1,* edited by Laura Boss and Stanley H. Barkan. Copyright © 1993 by Lips Press. Reprinted by permission of the editors, author, and translator.

Menashe, Samuel: "The Annunciation" is from *Collected Poems* published by The National Poetry Foundation of the University of Maine, Orono, Maine. Reprinted by permission of the author.

Merton, Thomas: "Cana" is from *Collected Poems of Thomas Merton.* Copyright 1946 by New Directions Publishing Corporation. Reprinted by permission of New Directions Publishing Corporation, and David Higham Associates.

Merwin, W. S. The excerpt from "The Prodigal Son" is from *Green with Beasts.* Copyright © 1955, 1956 by W. S. Merwin. Reprinted by permission of Georges Borchardt, Inc.

Milosz, Czeslaw: "Temptation," "Abundant Catch (Luke 5:4–10)," "With Her," "Lecture V," and "Readings" are from *The Collected Poems, 1931–1987,* first published by The Ecco Press in 1988. Copyright © 1988 by Czeslaw Milosz Royalties, Inc. Reprinted by permission.

Mistral, Gabriela: "Martha and Mary," translated by Doris Dana, is reprinted by arrangement with Doris Dana, c/o Joan Daves Agency as agent for the proprietor.

Mitchell, Stephen: "The Annunciation," "Vermeer," "The Parable of the Sower," and "The Good Samaritan et Al." are from *Parables and Portraits* published by HarperCollins. Copyright © 1990 by Stephen Mitchell. Reprinted by permission of the author.

Muir, Edwin: "The Killing" is from *Collected Poems.* Copyright © 1960 by Willa Muir. Reprinted by permission of Oxford University Press, Inc.

Nagy, Ágnes Nemes: "Lazarus" is translated by Frederic Will. Used by permission of the translator.

Nemerov, Howard: "Nicodemus" and "A Sacrificed Author" are reprinted by permission of Margaret Nemerov.

Owen, Wilfred: "At a Calvary near the Ancre" is from *The Collected Poems of Wilfred Owen.* Copyright © 1963 by Chatto & Windus, Ltd. Reprinted by permission of New Directions Publishing Corporation.

Pankey, Eric: "As We Forgive Those" is from *Heartwood.* Copyright © 1988 by Eric Pankey. Reprinted by permission of Simon & Schuster. "The Reason" and "The Confession of Cleopas" are from *Apocrypha.* Copyright © 1991 by Eric Pankey. Reprinted by permission of Alfred A. Knopf, Inc.

Parra, Nicanor: "New Sermons and Preachings of the Christ of Elqui (1979)," "The Anti-Lazarus," "Lord's Prayer," and "The Discourse of the Good Thief" are from *Anti-Poems.* Copyright © 1985 by New Directions Publishing Corporation. Reprinted by permission of New Directions Publishing Corporation.

Pasolini, Pier Paolo: "The Day of My Death" is from *New Italian Poetry, 1945 to the Present, A Bilingual Anthology,* edited by Lawrence Smith. Originally published by Einaudi in *La Nuova Gioventù.* Reprinted by permission of the Regents of the University of California and the University of California Press and the estate of Pier Paolo Pasolini.

Pasternak, Boris: "The Christmas Star," "The Miracle," "The Garden of Gethsemane," "The Evil Days," "Hamlet," and "Magdalene (I)" are translated by Nina Kossman. Reprinted by permission of the translator.

Pilinszky, János: "Passion of Ravensbrück" is from *The Desert of Love,* translated by János Csokits and Ted Hughes. Reprinted by permission of Anvil Press Poetry Ltd.

Plath, Sylvia: "Magi" is from *Crossing the Water.* Copyright © 1971 by Ted Hughes. Reprinted by permission of HarperCollins Publishers, Inc.

Prévert, Jacques: "Our Father" and "Last Supper" are translated by Jeffrey Fiskin. © Editions Gallimard 1949. Reprinted by permission of the publisher and the translator.

Quasimodo, Salvatore: "Anno Domini MCMXLVII" is from *Salvatore Quasimodo, Complete Poems,* translated by Jack Bevan. Reprinted by permission of Anvil Press Poetry Ltd.

Rilke, Rainer Maria: "Mary's Visitation," "The Olive Garden," "On the Marriage at Cana," "The Departure of the Prodigal Son," "The Raising of Lazarus," "The Last Supper," "Pietà," and "Mary at Peace with the Risen Lord" are translated by David Curzon, Lori Seibel, and Will Alexander Washburn. Reprinted by permission of the translators.

Robinson, Edwin Arlington: "Calvary" is from *Children of the Night* (New York: Charles Scribner's Sons, 1897). "Many Are Called" is from *Collected Poems of Edwin Arlington Robinson.* Copyright 1921 by Edwin Arlington Robinson, renewed 1949 by Ruth Nivison. Reprinted by permission of Simon & Schuster. "The Prodigal Son" is from *Collected Poems of Edwin Arlington Robinson.* Copyright 1932 by Edwin Arlington Robinson, renewed 1960 by Ruth Nivison and Barbara R. Holt. Reprinted by permission of Simon & Schuster.

Roethke, Theodore: "Judge Not" is from *The Collected Poems of Theodore Rothke.* Copyright 1947 by The University of the South. Used by permission of Doubleday, a division of Bantam Doubleday Dell Publishing Group, Inc.

Różewicz, Tadeusz: "Massacre of the Boys," translated by Adam Czerniawski, is from *The Burning Forest: Modern Polish Poetry,* edited by Adam Czerniawski (Bloodaxe Books, 1988). Reprinted by permission of Bloodaxe Books Ltd.

Senghor, Léopold Sédar: "Return of the Prodigal Son" is from *The Collected Poetry* (Charlottesville: Virginia, 1991). Reprinted by permission of the University Press of Virginia.

Simmons, James: "In the Wilderness" is from *Poems 1956–1986* edited by Edna Longley. Reprinted by permission of The Gallery Press.

Steele, Peter: "Cana" is from *Marching on Paradise,* Longman Australia Pty Ltd. Reprinted by permission of the publisher.

Szymborska, Wisława: "Born of Woman" is from *Sounds, Feelings, Thoughts.* Copyright © 1981 by Princeton University Press. Reprinted by permission of Princeton University Press.

Tekeyan, Vahan: "Sacred Wrath" is translated by Diana Der-Hovanessian and Marsbed Margossian. Used by permission of the translators.

Thomas, Dylan: "This Bread I Break" is from *The Poems of Dylan Thomas.* Copyright © 1967 by The Trustees for the Copyrights of Dylan Thomas. Reprinted by permission of New Directions Publishing Corporation and David Higham Associates.

Tsvetayeva, Marina: "And, Not Crying in Vain" is translated by Nancy Pollak. Reprinted by permission of the translator. "Bethlehem" is translated by Nina Kossman. Reprinted by permission of the translator. "The Fatal Volume" is from *In the Inmost Hour of the Soul: Poems of Maria Tsvetayeva,* translated by Nina

Kossman, Humana Press, Totowa, NJ 07512 (1989). "Magdalene" is from *After Russia,* translated by Michael M. Naydan and Slava Yastremski. Reprinted by permission of Ardis Publishers.

Vallejo, César: "Our Daily Bread," translated by James Wright, is from *Neruda and Vallejo: Selected Poems,* edited by Robert Bly, Beacon Press, Boston, 1971. Copyright © 1971 and 1993 by Robert Bly. Reprinted by permission of Robert Bly.

Vinokurov, Yevgeny: "The Mother of Judas," translated by Anthony Rudolph, is from *Post-War Russian Poetry,* edited by Daniel Weissbort. Reprinted by permission of the editor and the translator.

Weissbort, Daniel: "Mourning" is from *Inscription* (Cross-Cultural Communications, 1993). Reprinted by permission of the author.

Wilbur, Richard: "Matthew VIII, 28 ff." is from *Walking to Sleep: New Poems and Translations.* Copyright © 1969 by Richard Wilbur. Reprinted by permission of Harcourt Brace and Company.

Williams, William Carlos: "The Gift" and "IX, The Parable of the Blind" from "Pictures from Brueghel" are from *Collected Poems of William Carlos Williams, 1909–1939, Vol. 1.* Copyright © 1938 by New Directions Publishing Corporation and Carcanet Press Limited.

Winters, Anne: "The Mill-Race" originally appeared in *TriQuarterly,* a publication of Northwestern University. Reprinted by permission of the author.

Wright, James: "Saint Judas" is from *Saint Judas.* Copyright © 1959 by James Wright, Wesleyan University Press. Reprinted by permission of University Press of New England.

Wright, Judith: "Eli, Eli" is from *Selected Poems.* Copyright 1971 by Judith Wright. Reprinted by permission of Angus & Robertson, a subsidiary of HarperCollins Publishers (Australia).

Yeats, W. B.: "The Magi" is from *The Poems of W. B. Yeats: A New Edition,* edited by Richard J. Finneran (New York, Macmillan, 1983). "The Mother of God" is reprinted by permission of Simon & Schuster from *The Poems of W. B. Yeats: A New Edition,* edited by Richard J. Finneran. Copyright 1933 by Macmillan Publishing Company, renewed 1961 by Bertha Georgie Yeats. "Two Songs from a Play" is reprinted by permission of Simon & Schuster from *The Poems of W. B. Yeats: A New Edition,* edited by Richard J. Finneran. Copyright 1928 by Macmillan Publishing Company, renewed 1956 by Bertha Georgie Yeats. "The Second Coming" reprinted with permission of Simon & Schuster from *The Poems of W. B. Yeats: A New Edition,* edited by Richard J. Finneran. Copyright 1924 by Macmillan Publishing Company, renewed 1952 by Bertha Georgie Yeats. Two excerpts from "Calvary," reprinted with permission of Simon & Schuster from *Collected Plays of W. B. Yeats.* Copyright 1921 by Macmillan Publishing Company, renewed 1949 by Bertha Georgie Yeats.

Zavalniuk, Leonid: "I Love My Enemies" is translated by Magda Bogin. Used by permission of the translator.

NOTES ON THE POEMS

THE WORD MADE FLESH

Wisława Szymborska, "Born of Woman"
> The title of this poem comes from Galatians 4:4, "But when the fullness of time had come, God sent his Son, Born of a woman, born under the law. . . ."

THE ANNUNCIATION

William Butler Yeats, "The Mother of God"
> For a fascinating discussion of Yeats's drafts of this poem and his process of drafting in general, see Curtis Bradford, *Yeats at Work* (Carbondale: Southern Illinois University Press, 1965), pp. 114–127. The notebook entry that Yeats elaborated into the poem reads:

> > The Virgin shrinks from the annunciation. Must she receive "the burning heavens in her womb"? Looks at the child upon her knees at once "with love and dread."

> Bradford comments that the quotation marks Yeats placed around the two phrases "no doubt indicated that he intended to use them in the poem. He found a place for the first at the end of stanza 1, the last line of which, in all drafts as in the finished poem, reads 'The heavens in my womb.' The second phrase so marked was not used, but does express the central idea of the poem."

> Yeats's note on lines 1 and 2 of the poem reads:

> > In "The Mother of God" the words "A fallen flare through the hollow of an ear" are, I am told, obscure. I had in my memory Byzantine mozaic pictures of the Annunciation, which show a line drawn from a star to the ear of the Virgin. She received the word through the ear, a star fell, and a star was born.

THE MAGI

Boris Pasternak, "The Christmas Star"
> This and all other poems by Pasternak in the anthology are taken from the poems annexed to the novel *Dr. Zhivago*, where they are presented as poems written by the Zhivago character. Donald Davie has extended commentaries on each of the poems in his essay, "The Poems of Dr. Zhivago," in *Slavic Excursions, Essays on Russian and Polish Literature* (Chicago: The University of Chicago Press, 1990), pp. 139–244. On the poem "The Christmas Star," he writes: "the

office of the poet is likened to, or even identified with, the role of Christ" (p. 220).

THE TEMPTATIONS IN THE WILDERNESS

Zbigniew Herbert, "Mr. Cogito Tells about the Temptation of Spinoza"
In an essay entitled "Spinoza's Bed," in *Still Life with Bridle* (New York: The Ecco Press, 1991), p. 145, Zbigniew Herbert makes a final remark pertinent to the poem:

> The art of renunciation is an act of courage—it requires the sacrifice of things universally desired (not without hesitation and regret) for matters that are great and incomprehensible.

THE SERMON ON THE MOUNT

Jacob Glatstein, "How Much Christian"
Second stanza, second line: *Translators' note:* A Mishnah-Jew is a simple man whose learning goes beyond the Bible to reading the Hebrew Mishnah, but who does not reach the level of a scholar in the Aramaic Talmud.

THE DAUGHTER OF JAIRUS

Czeslaw Milosz, "With Her"
Author's note: In 1945, during the big resettlements of population at the end of World War II, my family left Lithuania and was assigned quarters near Danzig (Gdansk) in a house belonging to a German peasant family. Only one old German woman remained in the house. She fell ill with typhus and there was nobody to take care of her. In spite of admonitions motivated partly by universal hatred for the Germans, my mother nursed her, became ill herself, and died.

HEALING THE SICK

Philip Larkin, "Faith Healing"
I doubt if Philip Larkin had a specific biblical text in mind when he wrote "Faith Healing," so the poem is not, strictly speaking, in the midrashic genre of this anthology. But the last stanza shows the poet's attempt to understand the attraction and power of faith healing, and the sweep of the last few lines leads this reader, at least, to think of the vast historical continuity from what is being described back to its origins, which is the text I have placed opposite the poem.

THE PRODIGAL SON

Rainer Maria Rilke, "The Departure of the Prodigal Son"
For a brilliant prose meditation by Rilke on the parable, see the last section

of *The Notebooks of Malte Laurids Brigge*, Stephen Mitchell, trans. (New York: Vintage Books, 1990).

Elizabeth Bishop, "The Prodigal"
For an extensive meditation on the poem, see Peter Steele, *Expatriates: Reflections on Modern Poetry* (Melbourne: Melbourne University Press, 1985), pp. 20–33.

THE LAST DAY OF PUBLIC TEACHING

Boris Pasternak, "The Miracle"
Donald Davie, in *Slavic Excursions,* observes that, unlike the Gospel account, where

> Christ is angered by the fig-tree because he is hungry, in Zhivago's ac-
> count Christ's motive is harder to define: the hunger which the fig-tree
> cannot allay is metaphysical. . . . [T]he sterility which is exterminated is
> only partly outside the observer's mind. . . . [T]he word *chudo,* which gives
> the poem its title . . . means "miracle" but also, more generally, "won-
> der," "marvel." . . . This ambiguity . . . should have prepared us to see,
> in the solitary traveller here, a human poet no less than an incarnate
> God. . . . Metaphorically he can do all these things; for within the created
> world of a poem the creator's fiat is absolute (pp. 222–24).

Edwin Arlington Robinson, "Many Are Called"
While in Greek mythology, Apollo was the god of medicine, music, and prophecy, in Virgil's *Eclogues,* Apollo is the patron of poetry and music. This is presumably what Edwin Arlington Robinson had in mind.

William Butler Yeats, "The Second Coming"
For a discussion of Yeats's successive drafts of this poem, see Jon Stallworthy, chapter 1 in *Between the Lines: Yeats's Poetry in the Making* (Oxford: Oxford University Press, 1963). For an exposition on the meaning of the imagery and Yeats's sources, see A. Norman Jeffares, *A Commentary on the Collected Poems of W. B. Yeats,* (Stanford: Stanford University Press, 1968), pp. 238–244. Jeffares states that the poem combines the "second coming in Matthew 24 and St. John's description of the beast of the Apocalypse in Revelations" (p. 239). The material cited on pages 243–244, however, seems to indicate other sources for Yeats's beast, which certainly doesn't match the descriptions in Revelations 13.

Jorge Luis Borges, "Matthew XXV:30"
For an extensive meditation on the poem see Peter Steele, *Expatriates: Reflections on Modern Poetry* (Melbourne: Melbourne University Press, 1985), pp. 34–49.

GETHSEMANE

Boris Pasternak, "Hamlet"
Donald Davie, in *Slavic Excursions,* remarks that Pasternak "saw Shakespeare's *Hamlet* as 'the drama of a vocation,' life is not a field of experience to be crossed, but the path of a destiny to be found and followed" (p. 176). "Hamlet" is the first poem in the sequence at the end of *Dr. Zhivago.* Davie makes the point that the poem "Hamlet" established "from the start that, whereas the Christian must believe the Christ-story unique and unrepeatable, Zhivago sees it in an archetypal pattern reproduced in the life of the tragic hero Hamlet and to some extent reproduced in his own life also" (p. 238).

Rainer Maria Rilke, "The Olive Garden"
Stanza five refers to Luke 22:43.

Paul Kane, "Disciples Asleep at Gethsemane"
The last line of stanza three refers to Mark 14:51–52.

THE CRUCIFIXION

Ted Hughes, "A God"
Some of the imagery in this poem refers to John 19:28–37.

Anna Akhmatova, "Crucifixion"
Mary, the mother of Jesus, referred to in the second stanza, is mentioned in this context in John 19:25.

Paul Celan, "Tenebrae"
The imagery in the latter part of the poem refers to John 19:43, "Blood and water flowed out."

D. H. Lawrence, "Eloi, Eloi, Lama Sabachthani?"
Title: This transliteration is the version in Mark 15:34.
The poem was written in 1915, and the imagery is from the trench fighting in the First World War.

Dick Barnes, "Chuang Tzu and Hui Tzu"
Author's note: It is possible that Chuang Tzu—eponymous author of the Taoist classic, the Chuang Tzu Book—is a fiction. In the book he seems to have regarded himself as one: he says he woke up from a dream that he was a butterfly dreaming it was Chuang Tzu. Hui Tzu, on the other hand, is a verifiable historical personage, Prime Minister of Liang and a logical philosopher, one whom the book represents as being (what Chuang Tzu is not) consistent, holding firmly to the intellect while Chuang Tzu levitates on the imagination.
The most famous story about them is this. One day as they were walking across a dam on the Hao River, Chuang Tzu said:
"Look at them little fish darting around. That's what they really enjoy."
"You're not a fish, how do you know what they enjoy?"

"You're not me, how do you know whether I know or not?"

"I may not be you but you're a fish even less, and that proves my point."

"Let's go back to your original question. You asked how I know what the fish enjoy. Your question implies you knew I knew what they enjoy. The answer is: I know it by walking alone on this here dam."

Editor's addendum: With reference to Dick Barnes's poem: Like the rabbis of the Midrash, Chinese sages make use of puns quite often. All Taoist immortals can fly.

Wilfred Owen, "At a Calvary near the Ancre"
The third line in the final stanza refers to John 15:13, "There is no greater love than this . . ."

J. Kates, "No Altarpiece"
Lines three and four refer to John 19:25–27.

Daniel Weissbort, "Mourning"
Author's note on line 5: "*Eli, Eli [lama sabachtani?]*—My Lord, my Lord, [why hast Thou forsaken me?] [This is] one of the most mournful of Yiddish songs."
Editor's note: The poem is, strictly speaking, a midrash on Psalm 22, the first line of which is "Eli, Eli," which Jesus is quoted as having uttered. Apropos of this, it is interesting to note that Erich Fromm, in "Psalm 22 and the Passion," the appendix to his book, *You Shall Be as Gods* (New York: Fawcett Premier Books, 1969), argues that "the Gospel tells us that Jesus, when he was dying, recited Psalm 22" (p. 182); the whole of the psalm, not just the first line, since the rabbinic method of citation was to quote the opening phrase or line of the text cited. This assumes that the writers of the Gospels were using this method of citation, a plausible but unprovable assumption.

Anna Kamienska, "On the Cross"
Translators' note: This is the last poem in Anna Kamienska's notebook.

THE RESURRECTION

William Butler Yeats, from "Two Songs from a Play" (*The Resurrection*)
For an exposition on the meaning of the imagery and Yeats's sources, see A. Norman Jeffares, *A Commentary on the Collected Poems of W. B. Yeats,* pp. 284–92. See also Jeffares's notes in *Eleven Plays of William Butler Yeats* (New York: Collier Books, 1973). The final verse, from "Everything that man esteems" on, are "a praise of man, who goes on creating heroically despite the fact that all things pass away" (*Eleven Plays,* p. 240).

INDEX OF POETS

INDEX OF TITLES